SAVING SPEEDWAY

The Provincial League & The Southern Area League

IF AT FIRST YOU DON'T SUCCEED ...

Ivan Mauger 1957 – A struggle to succeed in the Southern Area League. (John Chaplin/John Somerville Collection.)

Ivan Mauger – 1963 and 1964 Provincial League Riders Champion. (John Somerville Collection.)

Ivan Mauger – World Champion. 1968, 1969, 1970, 1972, 1977, 1979. (John Somerville Collection.)

Philip Dalling and John Somerville

HALSGROVE

First published in Great Britain in 2020

British Library Cataloguing-in-Publication Data
A CIP record for this title is available from the British Library

ISBN 978 0 85704 348 1

HALSGROVE
Halsgrove House,
Ryelands Industrial Estate,
Bagley Road, Wellington, Somerset TA21 9PZ
Tel: 01823 653777   Fax: 01823 216796
email: sales@halsgrove.com

Part of the Halsgrove group of companies
Information on all Halsgrove titles is available at: www.halsgrove.com

Printed and bound in the UK by Bell & Bain, Glasgow

CONTENTS

FOREWORD

LEN SILVER, PROVINCIAL LEAGUE RIDERS' CHAMPION IN 1962

DURING the mid to late 1950s speedway was going through a lean time, partially because of the entertainment tax which took huge chunks out of the available money. Tracks were closing at an alarming rate and many riders had to forget the sport.

In 1959 Mike Parker joined with Reg Fearman and others to re-open some of the closed tracks, offering team places to the unemployed riders at pay rates well below the previous norm (ranging between 50p (ten shillings then) and £1 per point. To everyone's amazement, riders rushed to join in!

At such attractive (to promoters) rates, many extinct clubs re-started and formed the new Provincial League, which became an overnight success story. I had been absent from the sport for about 18 months, having broken an arm at Southampton, using the insurance money to get a start in the used car business. I decided to race again after taking a speedway bike in part exchange for a car, and doing a practice run at Rye House.

My good friend Vic Gooden invited me to join his team at Ipswich in the National League, which was full of the best riders in the land, the only ones who had not lost their jobs in the big shut down. With my ex-cycle speedway buddy Dennis Day (from the Stratford Hammers), we filled the reserve berths for the Witches.

Two other old rider friends, Wally Mawdsley and Pete Lansdale, re-opened Rayleigh (and later Exeter and New Cross) in the Provincial League. Vic Gooden allowed myself and Dennis to also ride for Exeter. I was reluctant, but decided to give it a try providing I was paid at the maximum rate of £1 a point. That was agreed and it started the most successful period in my racing career, as I quickly became the number one at the County Ground.

The Provincial League as a concept was a tremendous success, with good attendance figures and new clubs always wanting to join in. It paved the way for the birth of the British League in 1965 after a year in which the Provincial tracks ran outside of the control of the Speedway Control Board and the Auto Cycle Union (ACU).

Under the direction of Sir Hartley Shawcross, a former Solicitor General, the seven clubs left in the National League joined the Provincials to form a new division, the British League, with pay rates of £1.50p a point (thirty shillings then), way below what the top clubs had been paying but still within the budget for the Provincials. By then I had retired following a serious racing accident and had taken over the promotion at my local track at Hackney Wick in the East End of London.

It began almost 20 years of fun and enjoyment for me personally.

Len Silver

Len Silver, Provincial League Riders' Champion in 1962.

INTRODUCTION

THERE are two sharply contrasting narratives when it comes to recalling the state of British speedway in the mid- to-late 1950s.

The popular version holds that the sport had declined dramatically from its high point in the immediate post-war era and by mid-decade was merely clinging on for dear life. The glamour had departed, together with four out of the five London tracks which had traditionally formed the central core of the sport at its highest level in the UK. As tracks closed the most talented performers took the remaining team places, displacing steady if unspectacular journeymen riders who, especially in the North of England, lost their livelihoods, sold their equipment and retired.

A major factor in undermining speedway was a punitive level of entertainment tax, with speedway ludicrously taxed as a 'mechanical or none-live' sport, ignoring the fact that it depended on the skill of its riders.

Excessive taxation, the fall in attendances as people's post-war hunger for entertainment of any kind was replaced by a combination of growing prosperity and more comfortable homes with a television in the corner of the living room, is the widely accepted reason for the sport's troubles in the 1950s. But there is another, more positive point of view, favoured by a some people who were around and involved at the time.

Adopting a military-style metaphor, they hold that, faced with difficulties it was unable to overcome, speedway made an effective strategic retreat into a small but formidable number of strongholds, from Belle Vue in the North down through the surviving centres in the Midlands and East Anglia, to the fortress of Wimbledon in South London and the coastal outposts of Southampton and Poole.

The proponents of this theory argue that the ten or eleven National League tracks that continued to operate in one big league after the closure to league racing of Wembley in 1957 were promoted by solid business-like professionals and, for the most part, attracted crowds which were of an order simply unimaginable to younger supporters today.

Continuing the metaphor, they add that every military organisation needs training units and speedway in the 1950s had the Southern Area League, which provided a steady stream of young riders and satisfied the needs of spectators who enjoyed Sunday afternoon racing in relaxed rural surroundings.

With the end of the harsh entertainment tax in 1957, speedway promotion again became an attractive proposition and would-be promoters across the country applied for licences to re-open closed venues. Instead of being welcomed by the sport's authorities, the newcomers were often treated with considerable suspicion and hostility by the men who had kept their tracks alive through the dark years and were resentful of those they believed were attempting to cash in on the more favourable financial climate.

Public response to revivals in centres including Liverpool, Bradford, Cradley Heath, Bristol, Exeter, St Austell and Plymouth between 1957-59 encouraged aspiring promoters to go further than staging challenge matches and individual events and consider forming a new league. Their plans were regarded with scepticism at the time, but their vision is honoured today.

Saving Speedway describes how the sport in Britain survived outside the National League system, and goes on to explore how both the new Provincial League promoters and those who had worked hard to provide racing opportunities through the Southern Area League overcame the obstacles they encountered. By the mid-1960s the PL boasted more than twice as many tracks as its senior counterpart, which was in terminal decline.

As relations worsened, the Provincial promoters found themselves labelled as rebels and were forced to operate outside the umbrella of Control Board and the overall governing body, the Auto Cycle Union (ACU). Fortunately, common sense eventually prevailed and the two leagues merged, heralding the British League and a new era of prosperity.

Philip Dalling
North Devon 2020

The skill the taxman denied ...

When legislating for a new entertainment tax in the 1940s, Britain's lawmakers foolishly defined speedway as a 'mechanical, non-live sport', ignoring the fact that everything depended upon the skill of its riders. This skill is apparent in this splendid action shot, as Jim Bond (right) of Wolverhampton lays down his machine to avoid the falling Bill Andrew of Poole. (Jim and Janet Bond.)

ACKNOWLEDGEMENTS

AS was the case with my four previous speedway books, the pleasure in researching and writing *Saving Speedway* stemmed largely from the enjoyable conversations I enjoyed with a great many people connected with the sport, who were unfailingly generous with their knowledge and opinions.

I have greatly enjoyed working closely with my collaborator, John Somerville, whose collection of speedway photographs, reflecting the work of the greatest photographers to have worked within the sport, is renowed worldwide.

A debt of gratitude is owed to many of the riders, journalists and administrators who were active in speedway in the 1950s and 1960s. Without their assistance the book would not have been possible. Special thanks to Len Silver for his foreword, Reg Fearman, for a postscript and for never appearing to tire of my many queries, to Peter Morrish for his great knowledge of the era, and to Eric Hockaday, for his wonderful memory and constant encouragement.

I also acknowledge valuable help from the following riders (and members of their families), journalists and speedway researchers, who are listed alphabetically. They have recalled the Provincial League and Southern Area League eras, have loaned photographs and memorabilia and given me the benefit of their deep knowledge of speedway. They have made a huge contribution, for which I am most grateful.

Richard F Austin, Robert Bamford, Mike Broadbank, Sally Chandler, Ted and Mavis Connor, Keith Corns, Joan Craven, Ray Cresp, Brian Crutcher, Gordon Day, Ray Day, Reg Duval, Bert Harkins, Jim Henry, Tracy Holmes, Ian Hoskins, Mike Hunter, John Hyam, Matthew Jackson, Howard Jones, Mike Kemp, Brenda and Leon Leat, Ken Mellor, George Major, Neil Middleditch, Roy Peacock, Andy Povey, Norman Redmond, John Skinner, Terry and Jean Stone, and the historians and statisticians, too many to name individually, of Speedway Researcher and other groups.

Finally, my thanks for much assistance and patient understanding to Brenda Dyer, my companion on visits to all but one of Britain's speedway venues. We have yet to cross the water!

To anyone I have inadvertently missed from the list above, my sincere apologies.

Chapter 1

TRUE GRIT KEPT SPEEDWAY ALIVE IN THE NORTH

IT has become fashionable, among those who have yet to discover its breathtaking scenery and friendly natives, to contend that 'it's grim oop North!'

Considered from the point of view of speedway racing in the mid- to late-1950s, it was a pretty fair claim to make. For the 1951 total of a round dozen league tracks in northern England and across the border in Scotland had shrunk to just two by the middle of the decade.

This is the story of how speedway survived in the North during those difficult years, followed by a separate chapter considering the situation in Scotland where, at least as far as league racing was concerned, the close-down was complete by the end of 1954.

When league racing began in 1929 two separate competitions were established, the English League (for teams in the North) and the Southern League. Each competition lasted for three years until the surviving tracks were merged into one National League.

Northern grit personified. Yorkshireman and 1930s Belle Vue star Frank Varey later promoted at Sheffield and is pictured watering the Owlerton track against a harsh industrial background of a spoil heap and a power station. (John Somerville Collection.)

The Southern League was a relatively stable affair but the English League, which in 1930 was renamed the Northern League, was chaotic.

In its first year the English League had no fewer than 18 starters, half as many again as the Southern League, reflecting the initial enthusiasm for the dirt track sport in the industrial cities and towns of Lancashire, Yorkshire, Staffordshire and the North-East. The Red Rose county produced the largest number of starters, with Manchester White City, Belle Vue, Warrington, Burnley, Bolton, Preston, Rochdale, Salford and Liverpool.

Yorkshire came next, with Leeds, Halifax, Sheffield, Barnsley and Middlesbrough, whilst Newcastle represented the North East. Hanley (Stoke on Trent) and Long Eaton (Derbyshire) arguably qualified by dint of being north of the River Trent, whilst Leicester, although in the northern competition, was well to the south of that river.

Controversy (and resignations) dogged the English League from the start. Manchester White City won the league on the track but then resigned following a dispute among promoters. Neighbours Belle Vue had resigned earlier in the season, together with Burnley, Bolton and Hanley (Stoke-on-Trent). Warrington, meanwhile, had been expelled from the competition whilst Long Eaton entered the league but did not race any matches! In the end Leeds were awarded the championship title, heading a league table in which clubs had raced an uneven number of matches, varying from 18 to 24.

In contrast, in the Southern League in 1929 just one club resigned mid-season and the eleven finishers all completed their scheduled fixtures.

The English League necessarily became the Northern League in 1930 with the arrival of Edinburgh (Marine Gardens) and Glasgow White City. At the end of the season the fixtures were again far from complete, with matches raced ranging from nine to the 21 completed by the eventual champions, Belle Vue.

With speedway's initial boom already beginning to decline, the Northern League in 1930 had just six finishers. Belle Vue were champions, ahead of Leeds, Sheffield, Leicester Super, Preston and Glasgow White City. Again, the fixtures were not completed.

When the teams lined up for the start of the first National League season in 1932 only two were from the North, Belle Vue and Sheffield, whilst the Scottish tracks had

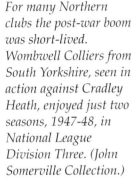

For many Northern clubs the post-war boom was short-lived. Wombwell Colliers from South Yorkshire, seen in action against Cradley Heath, enjoyed just two seasons, 1947-48, in National League Division Three. (John Somerville Collection.)

withdrawn. For the rest of the 1930s, although there was some open licence activity in the North and in Scotland, only Belle Vue, Sheffield, Nottingham, Liverpool, Newcastle and Leeds intermittently kept the Northern flag flying.

The fateful year of 1939 brought a northern revival. Belle Vue, the only side from the North in the top tier of league speedway for much of the time, won their fifth National League title of the decade. In National League Division Two, formed in 1938 to replace the original Provincial League (1936-37) the North dominated, with Newcastle clear champions ahead of Sheffield. On the debit side, Stoke (replaced by a Belle Vue reserve team) and Middlesbrough, along with Southerners Crystal Palace, resigned mid-season. Both Edinburgh (Marine Gardens) and Glasgow White City took part in 1939 in a subsidiary competition, The Union Cup.

Belle Vue famously never closed despite World War Two, and one or two other northern tracks – Glasgow White City, the new venue at Bradford Odsal, Middlesbrough, Newcastle and Sheffield ran on open licences in 1945.

When two divisions, each with six clubs, re-started league racing in 1946, half were from the North and Scotland. In the National League Belle Vue fans once again had a Roses Match to look forward to, with Bradford Odsal taking its place in the top tier. The four other clubs, Wembley (champions), Wimbledon, New Cross and West Ham, were all from the metropolis, which had similarly dominated the top division pre-war.

The second tier, named (for 1946 only) the Northern League, in fact had just three teams from the North of England – champions Middlesbrough, Sheffield and Newcastle – with the other participants being Norwich, Birmingham and Glasgow White City. As the league structure increased to three divisions, the peak of 12 clubs from the North/Scotland was reached in 1951. Division Two in particular was a North of England and Scottish stronghold, with ten of the 18 starters coming from the region or from north of the Border.

Sadly, speedway's northern decline started early. Wigan ran for just one Division Two season in 1947 and Wombwell Colliers closed at the end of the 1948 season.

When speedway in the North went into steep decline Manchester's Belle Vue and its training school became an even greater magnet than ever before for young hopefuls. Pictured with Aces manager Miss Alice Hart are Dennis Jenkins (later of Bradford and Sheffield) and Belle Vue's Peter Williams. (Author's Collection.)

Roy Peacock, who rode for Liverpool in the Provincial League before becoming a dance band singer, was a product of Belle Vue's Training School. (Photo Roy Peacock.)

Sheffield and Newcastle quit Division Two at the end of the 1950 and 1951 campaigns respectively. Liverpool and Ashfield resigned at the end of 1952 and with withdrawals occurring in other parts of the country as well, the second tier in 1953 was down to nine clubs, of which three were the surviving Scottish teams, Edinburgh, Motherwell and Glasgow White City, four from the Midlands in champions Coventry, Wolverhampton (which had by then swallowed up Cradley's licence racing), Leicester and Stoke, with Poole and Yarmouth making up the numbers.

By this point the writing was on the wall for speedway as a whole and after a wet summer in 1953, things began to go badly wrong in 1954. The Southern League (formerly the National League Division Three) effectively merged with Division Two and embarked on the new season with 15 clubs. Travelling had always been an expensive item for clubs in Division Two, which over the post-war years developed a much greater geographical spread than Division One or Division Three/Southern League. Four clubs resigned in mid-season; the troubles experienced by Edinburgh and Glasgow White City are examined in the Scottish review at the end of this chapter, and they were joined by Wolverhampton and Plymouth.

In Scotland Motherwell were left as the only team and it was no surprise when they did not resurface for 1955, when Belle Vue and Bradford were left as the only Northern tracks in operation.

At this point it is time to put the story of the league racing structure to one side and examine how those Scottish and Northern riders who decided to try and carry on in the sport rather than retire and sell their equipment managed to keep their interest intact. Former *Speedway Star* editor John Hyam has estimated the number of riders who did retire as being in the region of 500.

Speedway survived in the North and in Scotland in some fascinating guises and in some unlikely venues, including on the firm sands of Lancashire's Irish Sea coastline, on a former rubbish tip in Greater Manchester and at a Scottish agricultural showground, under the patronage of a noble Duke. The role played by speedway's closest neighbour in the world of motorcycle racing, grass tracking on more or less oval circuits, also played a major role in keeping the interest of riders alive, North and South of the Scottish border.

Most of all, speedway in the northern half of Great Britain survived due to the native grit, determination and humour of its inhabitants.

Fans often fought hard to try and keep speedway alive, after promoters decided the finances no longer added up. Fighting funds were sometimes launched but falling crowds and high taxation proved too great an obstacle.

Younger readers will marvel at the fact that tracks folded with average attendances in the 4000-5000 range, a figure British speedway today sees only for special meetings in the World Cup/British Championship sphere.

Attendances in the '50s did vary considerably and closures took place at the same time as other tracks were putting out house full signs.

Middlesbrough forms an interesting case study of a track where an excess of success is held to have caused closure. The Bears enjoyed considerable post-war success, including back to back title wins in the Northern League and National League Division Two in 1946 and 1947, but constant runaway victories eroded attendances. Football fans rarely object to their team winning by several goals, but runaway victories in speedway can empty stands and terraces.

The Bears' team moved to Newcastle for 1949 and would-be replacement promoters at Cleveland Park were refused an open licence. All was not lost on Teeside however, as

Speedway's flame was kept alive in the North by training tracks and grass track racing. Starting line action above from Ainsdale Sands, on Lancashire's Irish Sea Coast, which attracted spectators in large numbers. (Photo Roy Peacock.)

Grass track racing was a traditional route into speedway and meetings in Yorkshire attracted large crowds. A Yorkshire Post photographer was at Esholt near Bradford in 1957 to capture Ken Mellor ahead of the field. The photograph was seen by Oliver Langton who ran Belle Vue's training school and Ken was duly invited for a trial. (Photo Ken Mellor.)

At Clifton Park, Rotherham on Bank Holidays interest was so high that the afternoon meeting was repeated in the evening. The Payling brothers from the South Yorkshire coalfield are pictured in the pits. Maurice 'Slant' Payling, (centre) went on to enjoy success as a Belle Vue rider. (Photo Payling family.)

in 1953 Middlesbrough and District Motor Club staged a season of what was termed dirt track meetings at the track and continued to run meetings until at least 1956, providing plenty of opportunities for under-employed speedway riders and northern grass trackers.

The first known Middlesbrough amateur meeting, on 24 August 1953, for the Richard Wake Trophy was won by the vastly experienced Jack Hodgson who, with elder brother Frank, had been a key member of Middlesbrough Bears' teams in the post-war years. Other speedway men taking part in the meeting included Middlesbrough-born Peter Lloyd, who raced for his home town team, Newcastle and Glasgow Ashfield and Maurice Tate, who later spent many years as the start marshal at Cleveland Park.

The Middlesbrough years in the mid-1950s is a rarely explored aspect of the sport's history and the author is indebted to Ken Mellor, proud Yorkshireman and lifelong all-round motorcycle enthusiast, who rode speedway at Aldershot and Southampton in the early 1960s. Ken, whose own book, *Only Bounders Ride Motorcycles – 100 Years of Family Motorcycling* (ISBN 9781526206671) contains a great deal of interest for speedway and grass track fans, recalls:

I was present at a meeting at Cleveland Park in July 1956 acting as mechanic for Dave Giles who, like Peter Lloyd, was a rival of mine on Northern grass track circuits. I rode myself at the Middlesbrough club's next dirt track meeting at Cleveland Park, on my grass track bike. My first experience of speedway had been at Bradford in 1949 and I was a regular at Odsal until the track closed in 1957.

Across the Pennines in Manchester Belle Vue was the magnet that drew young northern hopefuls who, despite a lack of operating tracks in the region, still dreamed of professional speedway careers.

When speedway re-started in 1945 Johnnie Hoskins was squeezed out of his pre-war interest in West Ham. He first of all launched Bradford Odsal and then had promoting interests in Scotland. In 1953 he was back in Division One, replacing another speedway legend, Miss Alice Hart, as manager at Belle Vue. The Hyde Road complex, with its fun fair, zoo and other attractions, promoted itself as 'The Showground of the World' and the appointment of speedway's top showman seemed to be a marriage made in heaven.

Belle Vue already had a training school in operation and had nurtured new post-war stars such as Ken Sharples and Louis Lawson and were soon to see the rise to fame of diminutive Liverpudlian Peter Craven. But with skipper Jack Parker ageing and the Aces slipping from second place in the league in 1951 to mid-table a year later, Hoskins was under pressure to unearth a constant supply of home grown talent. He continued the training school but also revitalised the Hyde Road second halves, introducing the famous 'Bubble Bounce' handicap races for juniors.

There were usually two heats, each with five riders, and these offered opportunities to shine for many hopefuls who were later to appear in the Belle Vue National League team and also shine in the Provincial League. On a typical Saturday night at Belle Vue in May 1954, when the Aces rode against cross-Pennine rivals Odsal, the 'Bubble Bounce' races featured Tony Robinson, Bryce Subritsky, Brian Craven, Peter Williams, and Slant Payling, all of whom were to wear Aces colours in the National League.

At the start of the 1954 season a full meeting was staged, a rare opportunity for juniors to experience real competition in a match setting. Belle Vue Juniors took on a side from the newly-formed Southern Area League, Brafield Flying Foxes, losing by four points to the Northamptonshire team. The Aces Juniors included Payling, Derek 'Tink' Maynard, Graham Beattie, Ron Houlston, Ted Howell, Des Haswell, Tommy Toll and Norman Redmond – the last three more usually associated with Bradford Odsal. Two members of the Brafield side, Eric Eadon and Clive Featherby went on to succeed in the Provincial League.

Like many other aspiring speedway riders, Ken Mellor's opportunity to join the Hyde Road training school came through grass track racing. He competed in an Easter Monday meeting near Bradford in 1957 when a photographer from the *Yorkshire Post* newspaper arrived, looking for a picture depicting Bank Holiday sport. His shot of Mellor leading the pack was good enough to feature on the front page of the *Post's* sister evening paper the next day and was spotted by Belle Vue trainer Oliver Langton.

Langton liked Ken's style and offered him a chance to show what he could do on a speedway track. Ken remembers:

> After doing some laps of the Belle Vue circuit I was waved down to the starting line. As the tapes were not working it was a question of starting in my own time. It was my moment of truth. Either I would make an impression or fall flat on my face. I tended to drift out towards the safety fence but when I returned to the pits gate the starting marshal recognised the problem and told me to open out the throttle when I felt I was losing the front wheel.

> The next few laps got better and better, although I soon realised that there was no comparison with cornering on grass.

Ken's sessions at Hyde Road became known and caused problems in grass track

When Middlesbrough closed to professional speedway a local motorcycle club organised racing for several seasons in the mid-1950s. Many established and aspiring speedway riders competed, including Ken Mellor, who went on to ride for Aldershot and Southampton. (Photo Ken Mellor.)

THE
MIDDLESBROUGH AND DISTRICT MOTOR CLUB
present
THE SEVENTH DIRT TRACK
MOTOR CYCLE RACE MEETING
under the General Competition Rules of the A.C.U. Permit No. E.Y. 440.

GUILDHALL POLICE DOGS

AT CLEVELAND PARK STADIUM
MIDDLESBROUGH

THURSDAY, 26th JULY, 1956, at 7-30 p.m.

PROGRAMME ... SIXPENCE

circles. Rumours of his experiences on an actual speedway track spread and some fellow grass trackers believed this should exclude him from their meetings. The objection was over-ruled on the grounds that practicing at the training school hardly comprised professionalism.

Following a route well trodden by British hopefuls, Ken signed up with the Claude Boston 'circus' which presented speedway of a basic nature in France, helping him win contracts with Aldershot and Southampton.

Belle Vue and Johnnie Hoskins had a part to play in one of the saddest stories to emerge from northern speedway in the 1950s. Liverpool Chads (the team was named after a cartoon character) closed in August 1953 as crowds diminished at the Stanley Stadium.

In the period 1955-56 Hoskins, always on the lookout for additional opportunities for the large number of juniors clamouring for rides at Hyde Road, showed interest in re-opening at Stanley as a feeder to Belle Vue. The intention was to run open licence meetings and training sessions, with the longer term aim of applying for league status for 1957. Why the project failed to go ahead is not clear.

There was, however, to be speedway on Merseyside in 1957, as Richard Austin, a Liverpool speedway fan who now lives in California, explains:

> A small note in the *Liverpool Echo* indicated that former Chads' rider Reg Duval was to promote speedway at the Stanley track with the first meeting scheduled for Easter Monday. The report said that Reg was in the process of contacting both Split Waterman and Brian Crutcher, big names with fan appeal, who happened to be available at the time.
>
> I attended the first meeting and remember vividly that prior to the opening ceremony Reg walked around the entire track waving to the crowd; the spectators loved him as an ex-Chad bringing speedway back to the City.
>
> Initial response was excellent and prospects seemed good. Former Chads' rider and Liverpudlian Peter Craven won the Liverpool Easter Trophy from a field comprising National League riders such as Arthur Wright of Bradford, Jim Lightfoot of Coventry, and a roster of Northern juniors and second strings. The speedway press reported that the attendance was in the region of 11,000 people. By the time of the closure this had been reduced to around 4000, according to the *Liverpool Echo*.

Richard Austin recalls that he was 'shocked and disappointed' when the promotion folded in early June, after just seven meetings. The angry and frustrated Duval chose *Speedway and Stock Car World* as the platform to let loose both barrels at those he blamed for the closure, saying:

> I am quite sure that Liverpool would still be operating if it wasn't for the attitude of certain promoters and the Promoters' Association. They made things as difficult as possible for an open-licence track to hold meetings, by imposing restrictions and conditions on the booking of riders.
>
> The first of these was to charge a booking fee for riders and even then not let a rider ride in two consecutive meetings. After a couple of weeks, at the next Promoters' Association meeting, some more conditions were added. They would not allow a full league team to come to Liverpool.

After initial opposition from Wimbledon chief Ronnie Greene, the most powerful man in British speedway at the time, Duval won a grudging agreement from the National League Promoters' Association that he could attend a meeting to put his case. Reg told the *World*:

> That meeting certainly proved to be an eye-opener and I learned the true reasons for the opposition to new tracks opening. A few promoters – the ones who had the most to say – were definitely against anyone making a profit by opening a track now that entertainment tax has been abolished. They also complained that there are not enough riders available and did not want to risk a rider getting injured on an open licence track.
>
> Apparently these promoters do not realise that the main reason why riders are dropping out of the sport is because there are insufficient meetings to make speedway racing a full time occupation.

Opposite: Slant Payling before competing in the Belle Vue 'Bubble Bounce' event. (Peter Morrish/ John Somerville Collection.)

The North East also had a training track, with a surface of power station ash at Aycliffe, in County Durham. Greyhound and stock car racing were staged there until 1989. (John Somerville Collection.)

Duval absolved Johnnie Hoskins and Belle Vue from his complaint about the attitude of 'certain promoters', saying: 'One track to benefit by the revived interest in Liverpool was Belle Vue, and Johnnie Hoskins, realising it, was all in favour of his riders racing there'.

Liverpool supporters had become dissatisfied with having a changing team line-up each week, without any riders they could look upon as their own and Duval added:

The Promoters' Association would not even consider allocating riders to Liverpool and allowing them to participate in the league. Consequently attendances started to drop. It takes a lot to regain lost support and as there was no indication that this would be possible, I decided to cut my losses and close. Had I not had to pay a couple of hundred pounds in booking fees to other promoters in that short period, I would have been prepared to continue holding meetings with the hope that conditions would change.

Reg Fearman, one of the sport's foremost promoters and administrators in later years, can see both sides of the argument in the case of Liverpool in 1957.

No promoter wants to risk the safety of his valuable riders – and possibly the survival of his own track – by allowing them to race for other concerns. A prime example happened to me at Long Eaton in 1964 when my captain Ken Adams and Ray Wilson, just starting to really come into his own as a teenage sensation, accepted bookings at open licence track Weymouth.

Ken Adams fell in front of Wilson and Ray naturally steered away from his fallen team-mate and hit a fence post, breaking a femur. Adams was unhurt but Ray, a real crowd favourite at Station Road and with scoring potential, was out for some time.

Fearman understands the attitudes of the National League promoters who had struggled through the darkest years but has some sympathy too for those who argue that the competition, with a viable membership varying between nine and eleven tracks in the late 1950s, most of them enjoying good crowds (Ove Fundin remembers 8000 spectators at Norwich at the time), had become a cosy, self-satisfied and exclusive club.

It was fine for those, either in management or in the pits, who were fortunate enough to be part of the club. For those trying to keep a foothold in the sport, or struggling to get their first break, the position was rather less rosy.

One graduate of the Belle Vue training school in the early 1950s, Roy Peacock, was a prime example of the determination needed by northern novices, forced to seek opportunities to practice and race in circumstances that must have seemed bizarre to their counterparts in the South accustomed to the availability of Rye House, Eastbourne and other venues.

Roy's father Arthur, also a racer, ran a motorcycle business in Manchester and his son's career was kick-started by an exchange deal with former Fleetwood rider Ernie Appleby, who had just constructed a training track at Newton Heath, Manchester. Appleby, who had retired from racing through injury, was looking for some reliable transport when he spotted a Brough Superior motorcycle combination in Arthur Peacock's showroom.

Arthur allowed Ernie to have the Brough – a machine which would be worth many thousands of pounds to collectors today – in exchange for a speedway Rudge with a JAP engine. Both Arthur and Roy Peacock shared this machine at Newton Heath, at Ainsdale Sands near Southport and at a private circuit established in 1947 in the Lancashire mining village of Copull, a small, bowl-shaped track built by former Northern Riders Champion Oliver Hart and his brother Ron.

Roy Peacock went on to drive a midget car for the Mike Parker stable and this connection won him rides in the 'Pirate' meetings of 1959 and a team place with Liverpool when Parker and Fearman opened Stanley Stadium for Provincial League racing. He recorded some promising scores in the early part of the season but then turned to a new occupation which was to bring him considerable fame. A talented vocalist, Peacock gave

Former rider Ernie Appleby opened a track on a former rubbish and ash tip at Newton Heath in Manchester which for some time was without a safety barrier. This group is pictured after a fence was constructed. Left to right in front of the barrier are Johnny O'Neill, Duggie Spencer, Bob Chew, Roy Peacock and Eric Smith. Standing, l-r, are Buck Whitby, promoter Ernie Appleby (on crutches), Mr Chew and Arthur Peacock. (Photo Roy Peacock.)

The piles of ash and waste are clearly visible as Roy Peacock broadsides around Newton Heath. (Photo Roy Peacock.)

More action amid the sand dunes at Ainsdale. (Photo Roy Peacock.)

For some years the action at Ainsdale was organised by World Champion Peter Craven (right) and his brother Brian, who also rode for Belle Vue. Pictured at Ainsdale with Peter's Jowett Jubilee car. (Craven family.)

When the punitive entertainment tax was lifted in 1957 former Liverpool rider Reg Duval brought racing back to the city's Stanley Stadium. Liverpool-born Peter Craven won the opening individual meeting and is pictured with the trophy, Reg Duval and Reg's wife, Norma. (Richard Austin.)

up the shale to take a place fronting the nationally known Sid Phillips Dance Band and eventually became internationally known for his Bing Crosby tribute act, for which he gained the approval of Crosby himself.

His memories of Newton Heath, and the at times frightening challenges the 320-yard track offered to riders, are vivid. Roy explained:

Speedway can be dangerous enough on a well-prepared and maintained track, with every possible safety precaution being taken. Newton Heath was literally a tip and it took some time after we started riding there for a safety fence to be erected. One corner of the circuit was perilously close to the edge of a steep dip in ground level and riders needed to be extremely cautious.

My father said that if you went too wide in the days when there was no fence, you would need a parachute. I know I had one or two close shaves on the turn and I was glad I had packed a spare pair of underpants!

Ainsdale Sands had its own hazards, of onrushing tides and swiftly-descending sea mists. The location, in speedway terms, is closely associated with the development of the career of Peter Craven, Belle Vue Ace supreme and a double World Champion, who died after a track crash at Edinburgh in 1963.

The circuit on the sands between Freshfield and Ainsdale, was developed by former Liverpool rider Charlie Oates in 1948. The 380-yard track was marked out with sandbags, and elastic

No. 618   Thursday, May 2nd, 1957   Ninepence

Liverpool opens—Craven wins

was used for a starting gate. Among the novices who flocked to Ainsdale were Brian and Peter Craven and the brothers later took over the organisation of the training, continuing long after Peter had become an international star.

At its peak Ainsdale attracted considerable crowds, particularly when it staged actual meetings. Bill Bridgett, future Stoke and Wolverhampton rider and promoter at Monmore Green, won the Winter Trainees Trophy in February 1950 and Brian Craven lifted the Ainsdale Supporters' Trophy.

Racing on the sands had its ups and downs, apart from tidal interruptions. The race strip laid out by Charlie Oates had been carefully chosen for its location a good way from any housing but later some novices broke away and practised on land close to built-up areas, leading to complaints of noise nuisance. Racing on a regular basis is believed to have ceased in the 1980s, although riders have continued on occasions to attempt to practice.

Speedway in the North of England was holding on by its bootstraps as the end of the '50s decade neared. It had been a struggle for those riders determined to either hold on to their existing careers or establish a foothold in the sport. But scarce as their opportunities had sometimes seemed, they had been relatively well off when compared to their counterparts in Scotland.

Chapter 2
FEAST AND FAMINE FOR TARTAN TRACKMEN

SCOTLAND has a long, distinguished, usually colourful and occasionally complicated speedway pedigree. Both in the earliest days of the sport and again in the decade following World War Two, speedway north of the border experienced times of feast followed by famine.

Dirt track action came first to Glasgow, some two months after the event at King's Oak Speedway, High Beech, widely (but not universally) regarded as Britain's first speedway meeting. The venue was the Nelson Athletic Grounds, a greyhound and trotting circuit. As the sport mushroomed, racing took place at no fewer than four venues in Glasgow, with purists contending that the first *real* Scottish speedway took place at Glasgow Celtic FC's Parkhead ground three weeks later.

Their argument is based on the fact that Celtic Park had a proper cinder track, unlike Nelson. Pioneer Scottish rider/promoter Norrie Isbister also favoured Parkhead's case on the grounds that Nelson's circuit was egg-shaped, had bends of differing radii and was 'board hard', with competitors racing with feet up on their footrests. He also argued that the machines used were not stripped down but ridden in road trim.

In 1928, in addition to Celtic Park and Nelson Athletic Grounds, there were two more Glasgow venues, at Carntyne Greyhound Stadium and the White City Stadium.

Edinburgh's first taste of speedway came in May, at Marine Gardens, an entertainment complex on the shores of the Firth of Forth, which following World War One included a stadium used for football, greyhound racing and later speedway. Outside the two main centres of population, a track at Airbles Road in Motherwell operated between 1930 and 1932.

Scotland's proud speedway heritage dates back to 1928, in both Glasgow and at Marine Gardens in Edinburgh, pictured above. (John Somerville Collection.)

The Hoskins family, headed by Johnnie (pictured wearing the tartan) had an interest in Glasgow White City, Glasgow Ashfield and Edinburgh in the post-World War Two period. (Peter Morrish/ John Somerville Collection.)

League speedway arrived in 1930, when the entry of Glasgow White City and a Marine Gardens team known simply as Edinburgh forced the English League to change its name to the Northern League. Marine Gardens scooped the honour of being the first track to stage league racing in Scotland, on 19 April, when Edinburgh lost by 21 points to 13 to Belle Vue in a six heat match with four man teams plus a reserve.

White City fans had to wait for three days for league action, starting with a 23-13 victory over Leicester Super. At the end of a season in which the fixtures were very far from completed, Edinburgh were ranked eighth out of 13 finishers, with Glasgow finishing tenth.

Marine Gardens reverted to open licence individual events in 1931 but White City again entered what was to be a much smaller Northern League, which began the season with six competing tracks but ended it with just four. White City and Leicester Super withdrew mid season but their results were retained in the league table. The Glasgow side was again in last place, with Leicester Super just above them.

With speedway nationally entering its first decline, both Edinburgh Marine Gardens and Glasgow White City closed at the end of the 1931 season. For seven long years speedway racing was more or less extinct in Scotland. Signs of revival came in 1937 when northern riders Rol and Maurice Stobbart from Cumbria promoted two meetings at Dam Park, Ayr. Much later, in 1949 and nearing the end of their track careers, both brothers made appearances for Glasgow's Ashfield Giants.

Marine Gardens was the first to re-emerge, running successfully on an open licence in 1938, staging challenge matches against a variety of English opponents and a team made up of Australians racing in Britain. The venue also featured a midget car meeting.

Edinburgh came to the tapes again for 1939 and Johnnie Hoskins also re-opened Glasgow White City. A two-tier league structure had returned to speedway in 1936 and 1937 in the form of the original Provincial League. This was succeeded in 1938 by a National League Division Two and before the 1939 season got underway there were hopes that both Scottish tracks could be included.

At this point speedway politics intervened. Two English Division Two tracks, Hackney Wick in East London and Bristol, objected on grounds of travel costs. Even after three teams – Middlesbrough, Stoke and Crystal Palace – had withdrawn from the second tier mid-season there was still no place for the Scottish teams. A Belle Vue reserve team took over the fixtures of Stoke and Edinburgh and White City, both having begun the season on open licences, applied to fill the other vacancies but, again, travel costs worked against them.

The Scottish sides were nevertheless welcomed into a subsidiary competition, the Union Cup, placed in the Northern Section with Belle Vue Reserves, Newcastle and Sheffield, thus avoiding any further objections from the Southern tracks. Edinburgh raced eight matches in the north group, finishing third out of five in an incomplete table. Glasgow completed five group fixtures and were ranked last.

The lack of success of the Scottish sides in the competition meant that a potentially embarrassing position was avoided. The winners of the Northern and Southern Groups were to have met in a two-legged final and Hackney Wick won the southern section. The qualification of either Edinburgh or Glasgow could have revived the travel costs issue. As it proved, the outbreak of World War Two brought the competition to a premature close.

Glasgow White City was one of a select few tracks that staged speedway during World War Two. Ten meetings were staged between 11 August and 17 October 1940 and the Glasgow team rode two away matches, at Odsal, Bradford and Brough Park, Newcastle.

Regular speedway became possible again after the surrender of the German forces on 8 May 1945 and White City were at the forefront of the return in Scotland. A team representing Glasgow took to the track at the sport's newest venue, the vast rugby league arena of Odsal, Bradford on 11 August 1945 – four days before VJ Day, which marked victory over Japan and effectively brought the war to a final conclusion.

On VJ Day itself – 15 August – White City added to the festive atmosphere in the city and the nation by staging a speedway match between Glasgow and London. Between that date and the middle of October, White City staged an England-Scotland match, seven matches between Glasgow and various scratch teams, a Scottish Best Pairs Championship and Scottish Senior and Junior Championships.

The riders used for the meetings were drawn from the restricted pool of men available at a time when the country was still undertaking the transition to peacetime conditions. One name that was to recur in Scottish speedway in future years was that of New Cross star Ron Johnson.

Although an Australian test rider, Johnson was born in Scotland before emigrating and was the only rider with a Scottish connection in the Scotland side that beat England 54-53 at White City on 22 August 1945. He also won the Scottish Senior Championship at the venue's final meeting of the season on 17 October, recording a 12 point maximum. The Junior Championship was won, somewhat incongruously, by Norman Evans of Middlesbrough and Newcastle fame, who was aged 41 at the time! Contemporary reports speak of capacity crowds at White City in those first weeks of peace, a foretaste of the boom in speedway attendances to come.

When league racing resumed for the 1946 season two divisions emerged, each with six teams. The top tier, named the National League, comprised four of the London 'Big Five' in Wembley, West Ham, New Cross and Wimbledon, together with Belle Vue and the new team based at Odsal, Bradford, initially known as the Boomerangs – perhaps in tribute to their manager, Johnnie Hoskins, whose bid to return to the control of West Ham after the war had been thwarted by the duo of former riders Arthur Atkinson and Stan Greatrex.

Johnnie Hoskins' son Ian, after returning from RAF pilot training in Canada, managed Glasgow Tigers. The 1950 team line-up is, back row, l-r, Jack Hodgson, Frank Hodgson, Ian Hoskins, Alf McIntosh, Gordon McGregor. Front, kneeling, l-r, Norman Lindsay, Peter Dykes, Tommy Miller, Ken McKinlay. (John Somerville Collection.)

Above: *Scottish rivalry was intense and in 1949 Edinburgh Monarchs signed Australian Jack Young, who two years later became the first rider from speedway's second tier to win the World Championship. Young won the title again in 1952 after moving south to West Ham. The team pictured here is, back row, l-r, Harold Fairhurst, Danny Lee, Bill Baird, Dick Campbell. Front row kneeling, l-r, Eddie Lack, Clem Mitchell, Jack Young, Don Cuppleditch. (John Somerville Collection.)*

Below: *Johnnie Hoskins, ever the showman, sent motorcyclists parading through Glasgow's city centre to advertise his track at Ashfield. (John Somerville Collection.)*

Glasgow White City were in the second tier, the Northern League, together with Middlesbrough, Newcastle, Sheffield, Norwich and Birmingham. Although White City finished bottom, continuing the side's lack of league success which had started in the 1930s, the season was a success financially, such was the appetite of a speedway-starved audience.

This was the start of a golden age for British speedway in general and in particular for the sport north of the border. White City was joined by Edinburgh in 1948, Glasgow Ashfield in 1949 and Motherwell in 1950. For a brief but heady period Scotland had four league teams, with huge crowds, particularly for the many local derby matches and for international matches against England.

The racing at the four league tracks was not the only speedway activity in Scotland in the immediate post-war era. Open licence racing was staged in the Bothwell Castle estate area with training sessions interspersed with the occasional challenge match against similar venues such as Newtongrange. The track helped nurture the careers of many leading riders, notably Tommy Miller and Ken McKinlay. The Bothwell venture eventually moved, safety fence and all, to another training track at Chapelhall.

From 1948 to 1955 (with the exception of 1952 when an outbreak of foot and mouth disease meant cancellation) racing was staged at the Lanarkshire Farmers' Agricultural Society's annual show at the Hamilton Showgrounds, situated on the estate of the Duke of Hamilton. When league speedway was booming in Scotland the event was a pleasant diversion from the cut and thrust of the National League Division Two for those team men, mostly from Glasgow White City, Ashfield and latterly Motherwell who took part, racing team matches on a surface variously described as being composed of shale or ash.

Some of the great names of Scottish speedway took part in the earlier meetings, including Tommy Miller, Ken McKinlay and Gordon McGregor and in later years riders making their way in the sport, including the Templeton Brothers, Doug and Willie, and Jimmy Tannock also raced at Hamilton, along with many lesser known names drawn from speedway second halves and the very active Scottish grass track circuit.

Hoskins' publicity initiatives helped to pack Ashfield, with a massive crowd at this international fixture. The Scottish team, l-r, Willie Wilson, Tommy Miller, Jack Young, Don Cuppleditch, Merv Harding, Junior Bainbridge, Dick Campbell and Keith Gurtner. (John Somerville Collection.)

Big crowds at Ashfield brought problems for Johnnie Hoskins, who was forced by Glasgow Corporation to construct concrete terracing for 10,000 people, to replace unsafe cinder banks. The cost was later blamed for the track's closure. Pictured above, Hoskins supervises the pouring of the concrete. (John Somerville Collection.)

As the tents were pitched for the show in May 1954, Scottish speedway was in a fragile state. Glasgow Ashfield had withdrawn from Division Two at the end of 1952 (the track continued in 1953 on an open licence) and White City had quit the competition in April '54, collapsing after completing just two home fixtures (and four away matches) in a subsidiary competition, the Northern Shield. All six matches had resulted in defeats for the Tigers.

White City manager Ian Hoskins, now temporarily out of speedway and about to start work as a welfare officer with Rolls Royce in Glasgow, later recalled the circumstances of Tigers' closure, telling *Speedway News*:

Glasgow Tigers no longer exist and everybody must be wondering how it all happened. Let me make one point clear, the shut down idea was not mine. First of all, it must be realised that White City were lucky to have been able to open at all. It was only because of the local greyhound company coming in with us that we were able to proceed with our plans.

One of the conditions of the takeover was that both Tommy Miller and Junior Bainbridge be transferred to offset some of the heavy losses incurred in 1953. I was left to try to build a new team that would not be a disgrace and would continue to command support. Apart from the loss of Miller and Bainbridge, Peter Dykes and Don Wilkinson retired and the only answer was to build up with youth.

Hoskins went on to explain that for the first home meeting, on a cold, damp night, there were fewer than 5000 people in the stadium to see the Tigers heavily beaten by visitors Coventry. The following week, despite a local derby against Edinburgh (won by the Monarchs) the crowd was only slightly up on the previous week, but still below 5000. The promotion had lost more than £400 on the two meetings.

Despite his personal problems, and the criticism inevitably coming his way, Ian Hoskins made his way to the Hamilton Showgrounds on Saturday 14 May to see a team bearing the Tigers named take on a side racing under the name of Lanarkshire Eagles Select in the showground arena.

Taking in the atmosphere of what he described in his regular column in *Speedway News* as a 'carefree and gay atmosphere, with the odd kilt and tartan tammie visible among the crowds and girls in riding breeches', Hoskins mused that speedway racing must have looked very much the same when his father promoted racing at West Maitland, New South Wales in 1923. He added:

It was the farmers who inspired my father to introduce motorcycle racing as an additional attraction to the cattle judging items at the Maitland Show. Speedway was born on a showground and here we were in Scotland carrying on the old tradition.

At Hamilton the dressing room was a large tent and the pits were a sheep pen. The bladed track was well rolled and watered and comparatively smooth and a safety fence of wire netting, pinned on to stakes, set racing at the show above the normal run of grass track meetings in the country. As there was no starting gate, somebody had the bright idea of using the headlights of a car to start the races. The riders had to wait for the headlights to be dimmed before dropping their clutches.

Hoskins reported that the match was won 45.5 to 37.5 points by Glasgow Tigers, with Willie Templeton (12 points) and brother Doug (11) the stars and Gordon Mitchell and Red Monteith the top scorers for Lanarkshire, with nine points apiece. Tommy Miller ran

Until the bubble burst Scotland's speedways became synonymous with big crowds. The grandstand at Old Meadowbank was always full to capacity. (John Somerville Collection.)

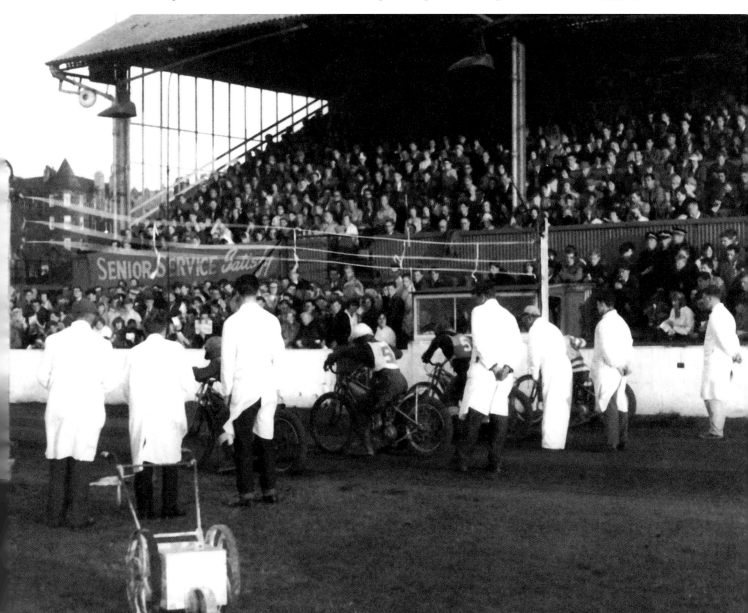

into the back of another rider, Johnny Reid, when Reid's chain came off. Miller's machine was badly damaged and he took no further part in the meeting. Ian concluded his article by saying:

> The crowds present at Hamilton Show were very little different in spirit from the time in West Maitland, 30 years or so ago, when a similar band of men and women cheered on their favourites to victory. Speedway may fade on the big-time scale, but in the end, as in the beginning, men will race for the love of the game long after the big money has been spent, and there will always be people to watch them.

It is not recorded if the Duke of Hamilton himself attended the speedway meetings which provided a grand finale each year for the shows held on his estate. Douglas Douglas-Hamilton, 14th Duke of Hamilton and 11th Duke of Brandon (1903 – 1973), a Scottish nobleman and aviator, was a character in his own right who was one of the first men to fly over Mount Everest.

There were more shocks to come for Scottish speedway fans in 1954. With the closure of White City the sport was now temporarily extinct in Glasgow, as open licence Ashfield did not re-emerge after the winter break. Now Edinburgh called it a day, with the final meeting at Old Meadowbank taking place on 10 July, when Ken McKinlay scored a perfect 15 point maximum to win the track's World Championship qualifying round.

Motherwell continued in National League Division Two until the end of the 1954 season, with the last meeting being run on 8 October, when the Eagles beat Ipswich 45-39.

Although the Scottish grass track scene continued to prosper, mainstream speedway had, with Motherwell's closure, entered a dark period. Until the birth of the Provincial League the only light to penetrate the scene came from brief revivals at White City in 1956 and Motherwell in 1958, and a student charity meeting staged at Old Meadowbank in 1959.

White City ran a short season of five matches in 1956, not particularly well attended, promoted by former Tigers' Tommy Miller and Junior Bainbridge. At Motherwell, the suggestion of a meeting for junior riders in 1955, had been shelved, reportedly because of a lack of interest from the riders! Training sessions were held at the track in 1957 and

Below left: Until he moved to West Ham Jack Young, pictured in Monarchs' colours, was one of the reasons for crowd enthusiasm at Meadowbank. (Peter Morrish/John Somerville Collection.)

Below right: Jimmy Cox was one rider who kept his interest in the sport alive during the dark days for Scottish speedway and was a link between the Monarchs of the early 1950s and the team for the first season of the Provincial League, in 1960. (Peter Morrish/ John Somerville Collection.)

in 1958 Ian Hoskins sought to supplement his income from industry by getting back into speedway.

The first of five meetings provided an opportunity for really competitive team racing for not just the surviving rump of Scottish riders but also for the visiting team, described as Belle Vue Babes and consisting of Hyde Road juniors. The Belle Vue hopefuls, despite all being accustomed to fairly regular second half opportunities, were outclassed by the Scottish riders whose chances on shale as opposed to on the grass, were much more limited.

Motherwell won the match 50-27 but the actual result is less interesting than other aspects of the occasion. The home team featured no fewer than five riders who were to form the core of the Edinburgh Monarchs first Provincial League team when league racing returned to Scotland. And the match will always be remembered for the speedway debut of a young hopeful who was to become one of the biggest names in Scottish and British speedway.

Motherwell 1952. Pictured, l-r, Derek Close, Jock Scott, Noel Watson, Scott Hall, Norrie Isbister (manager), Keith Gurtner, Will Lowther, Bluey Scott, with Gordon McGregor on the machine. (John Somerville Collection.)

Fife farming brothers Willie (left) and Doug Templeton, both with limited experience of league racing before the Scottish tracks closed in the period 1951-54, were leading grass track competitors who also took advantage of the brief revivals at Glasgow White City (1956) and Motherwell (1958). Both raced for Edinburgh in the first season of the Provincial League. (Peter Morrish/ John Somerville Collection.)

Grass tracker George Hunter had never seen or ridden speedway before taking part in Motherwell's 1958 revival. He went on to become a star performer for both Edinburgh Monarchs and Glasgow Tigers as well as several English teams in a career spanning more than twenty years. (Peter Morrish/John Somerville Collection.)

Motherwell was the last of the four Scottish league tracks of the post-World War Two period to open and the last to close at the end of 1954, re-opening briefly in 1958. This picture shows the derelict track amidst the industrial landscape of the former capital of Scottish steel production. (John Somerville Collection.)

Predictably, the Templeton Brothers, with some experience of National League speedway, contributed 19 points to the match, performances matched by 11 points from Northern junior Fred Greenwell, who in 1960 was to be the only Englishman in the Monarchs Provincial League side. But the story of the night was the discovery of George Hunter, a young Scottish grass track rider who had not even seen speedway before taking to the Motherwell track and scoring 11 points from five rides.

The Belle Vue team was not without potential of its own. Graham Beattie, who top scored with 10 points, had considerable second half experience whilst Derek 'Tink Maynard', was making his way in the National League when he was killed racing for the Aces at Norwich and Jack Kitchen was to become a major Provincial League star.

For the final match of the 1958 Motherwell season six of the riders in the Lanarkshire Eagles team – Hunter, the Templetons, Gordon Mitchell, Greenwell and Jimmy Tannock – went on to ride for

National pride. Scotland v England international clashes, including this match at Division Two level at Glasgow White City in May 1952, set the fans alight. Scotland won this match 61-46. Tommy Miller scored a six ride, 18 point maximum for the Scots whilst England's top man was Billy Bales of Norwich, with 14 points. (Author's collection.)

Edinburgh at the start of the Provincial League season two years later. The fact that Ian Hoskins could rely on what was more or less a ready-made team when he launched Edinburgh in 1960 says volumes for the spirit of the Scottish riders during difficult times for speedway.

Chapter 3
SUNDAY CHEER FOR THE SOUTH

WHILST emphasising in the previous chapter the grimness of much of the 1950s for speedway in the North of England and in Scotland, there is no intention whatsoever of suggesting that the state of the sport in the South, where the swift decline in popularity had been perhaps even more stunning, was an absolute bed of roses.

Speedway in London at its peak had been truly vibrant. The 'big five' tracks of National League Division One attracted huge audiences and the metropolitan venues reached out in all directions, with thousands of people from the surrounding home counties, North, South, East and West, travelling into the capital each race night.

When the sport's aggregate attendance peaked at eleven million in the late 1940s, it is no exaggeration to suggest that almost half of that figure attended the London tracks, including Division Two Walthamstow.

With such enthusiasm for speedway, allied to the development of cycle speedway racing from its bombsite beginnings to a well-organised sport, it is no wonder that a very significant proportion of riders, from team men to novices, originated from London and the South-East. An analysis of team strengths on the basis of riders' places of birth and residence at the start of the new Provincial League in 1960, will readily support this claim.

Speedway's decline really began to gather pace in 1953 with the loss, for one reason or another, of six tracks, including the crushing blow to the sport's reputation and morale of the closure of Division One New Cross. Division Two was already depleted before the 1953 season began, having suffered the loss of Oxford (who dropped down to the Southern League), the resignation of Ashfield and the effective closure of Cradley Heath, although their fate was announced as a 'merger' with neighbours and close rivals Wolverhampton. Another loss came mid-season when Liverpool withdrew.

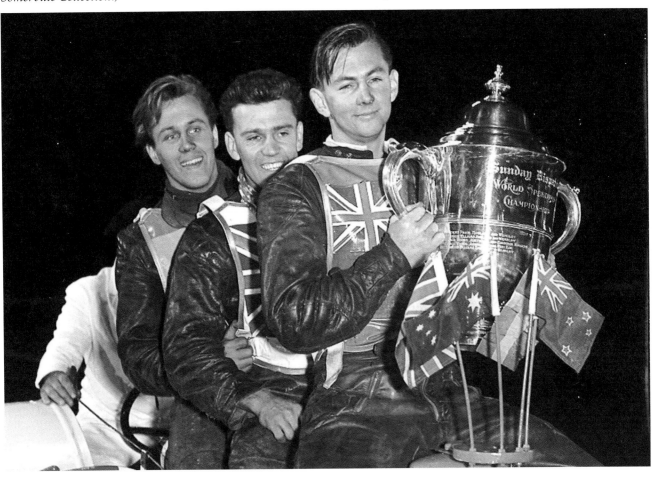

The Southern League, the successor in 1952 to the National League Division Three) had eleven tracks at the start of 1953 but finished Coronation Year with just eight, having lost Long Eaton, Cardiff, and Aldershot. It was the end for the three tier professional league system nationally. Of the eight surviving Southern League clubs seven linked up with the National League Division Two, with only St Austell choosing to quit league racing.

In the weeks before the start of the 1954 campaign Division Two looked likely to have a membership of 15 clubs, even though Yarmouth had been refused a racing licence for the season and Stoke Potters had withdrawn. Bristol filled one vacancy by stepping down from Division One and the acquisition of the former Southern League tracks potentially made for a healthy competition.

Things then started to rapidly go downhill. First Glasgow White City and Wolverhampton withdrew before the league fixtures began and the two tracks at the geographical extremes of the league, Edinburgh and Plymouth, pulled out, in the case of the Monarchs after five league fixtures, whilst Plymouth only raced one league match.

The creation of the Southern Area League in time for the 1954 season was a life-saver for many riders who otherwise would have stood precious little chance of being considered even for regular second half events at the remaining tracks in the South of England, let alone for increasingly scarce team places. Apart from the SAL, speedway in the true South in 1954 consisted of the four remaining Division One tracks – Wembley, Wimbledon, Harringay and West Ham, with Rayleigh and Southampton in Division Two. The second tier was very heavily weighted to the North and Midlands, Scotland and the South West.

Worse was to come both nationally and regionally. Harringay closed early in 1954, making way for the new phenomenon of stock car racing (first staged in the UK at New Cross). West Ham succumbed at the end of the 1955 campaign and Wembley in the winter of 1956-57, after the premature death of the Stadium's managing director, Sir Arthur Elvin.

When Divisions One and Two of the National League merged to form one league for 1957 the emphasis was again firmly on the English provinces - Belle Vue and Bradford in the North (Odsal taking over Birmingham's fixtures mid-season), Leicester, Coventry, Oxford and Swindon in the Midlands, Norwich and Ipswich in East Anglia, Wimbledon as the one surviving London track, together with Rayleigh, some 40 miles from the capital, and Southampton on the South Coast. Poole had temporarily dropped out of the league structure but ran in 1957 on an open licence and actually staged two of Rayleigh's National League fixtures at Wimborne Road.

July the fourth 1954 and the fans have turned out in force at Arlington Stadium to see the Eastbourne Eagles take on California Poppies in the Southern Area League. Eastbourne had for just one season staged professional league racing, when the Eagles won the National League Division Three in 1947. (Peter Morrish/John Somerville Collection.)

Rye House, based at Hoddesdon in Hertfordshire had been a renowned training track since the mid-1930s.
A feature was the corrugated iron safety fence visible in this action shot of Gil Goldfinch, who became one of the SAL's top men and also rode in the National and Provincial Leagues, and Les Nicholls.
(Peter Morrish/John Somerville Collection.)

John Wick, former editor of the *Speedway World* newspaper, who was later to play a major role in the formation of the Provincial League, had strong words to say about the state of the sport in the mid-to-late 1950s.

For some years the number of speedway leagues and teams showed an alarming drop. Yet despite warnings, nobody seemed prepared to do anything to stop the slide. Fewer new riders were coming into the sport, yet more and more experienced men were retiring. Only the Southern Area League offered any hope for newcomers but the cost of learning the art of speedway racing was high, with the prospect of returns very low.

A few National League promoters had made half-hearted attempts to encourage novices but the most they could offer was the chance of one or two second half rides. It was not surprising, therefore, that many of these newcomers soon lost heart and rapidly disappeared from the sport.

Throughout one of the most desperate periods speedway has ever faced, the Southern Area League was to prove a beacon for both riders and supporters. Those who still recall the period from personal experience look back on the SAL years with considerable affection. Regular competitive Sunday afternoon racing in pleasant and reasonably accessible (if often basic) surroundings certainly offered more opportunities than racing on an ash tip in Manchester or on the beaches of Lancashire.

The tracks which came together to form the Southern Area League in 1954, together with those which operated at various stages during the competition's five-season existence, were varied. Rye House and Eastbourne were the only two tracks to operate throughout the period of the SAL and as training centres and open licence tracks had been a stable and reliable presence on the speedway scene in the South for most of the sport's history.

Eastbourne staged an event in September 1928 and opened officially on August Bank Holiday Monday 1929. Arlington Stadium subsequently ran every year throughout the 1930s and managed to stage a meeting in 1940. It re-opened in 1946 and a year later became founder members and first champions of the new National League Division Three. Owner and pioneer rider Charlie Dugard, who had acquired the site of the stadium in the 1920s, then transferred the licence to Hastings and Eastbourne reverted to open licence status.

Rye House has almost as venerable a history as Eastbourne. The track, at Hoddesdon in Hertfordshire, 36 miles from central London and close to the River Lea Navigation, was originally a trotting circuit. It opened for speedway in the mid-1930s and in addition to offering facilities for training and practice, staged individual events and challenge matches, joining the Sunday Amateur Dirt Track League in 1938, competing against Eastbourne, Dagenham, Romford and Smallford. Rye House also staged speedway in the period 1940-43 inclusive, before taking a two year break until a resumption in 1945.

During the 1930s and on occasions during and after the war Rye House played host to top stars from the London clubs, and some teams hired the stadium for pre-season practice. The track at the time had a surface of black cinders and the safety fence, as is clearly visible from period photographs, was constructed from corrugated iron.

In the immediate post-war years former Australian test star Dicky Case acquired both the stadium and the adjacent Rye House pub. Sunday afternoon meetings, well attended by London speedway fans, were organised by George Kay, who promoted at Harringay for the Greyhound Racing Associaton (GRA). Around 1958 Rye House stadium was re-designed and a smaller speedway track located inside a greyhound track. While this re-construction was underway, a replacement speedway track was laid where the karting circuit now stands.

The massive contribution made by not only Rye House and Eastbourne in the immediate post-war period but by all the training circuits was the production of riders for the sport at a time when the talk was of a shortage rather than a glut of speed men.

Some sources have suggested that the Southern Area League replaced the former Southern League and, to a degree, the new competition can be viewed in that light. But none of the tracks that had competed in the Southern League in 1953 applied for admission to the new competition.

The third member of the SAL on the league's formation was Aldershot, where a track at Boxalls Lane had existed as early as 1929. In 1950 an Aldershot team entered National League Division Three, racing at Tongham Greyhound Stadium. The Shots continued in that section and in the successor Southern League until the end of 1952, and then reverted to an open licence for 1953, before linking up with the Southern Area League.

The other three founder members of the SAL, California Poppies, Ringwood Turfs, and Brafield Flying Foxes had only experienced open licence or training status in the years since speedway restarted after World War Two. Ringwood in the New Forest of Hampshire, and California, situated at Little California in England, near Wokingham in Berkshire, also had pre-World War Two pedigrees. The third, Brafield in Northamptonshire, the most northerly of the SAL clubs, first opened post-war for midget car racing.

The flavour of Southern Area League racing is captured in this action shot from California. It is notable for illustrating the close proximity of the crowd and the apparently flimsy nature of the safety barrier. (Author's Collection.)

Ringwood's location at Matchams Park was in easy reach of the South Coast's two speedway hotbeds, 18 miles from Poole and 22 from Southampton. The track staged speedway over three periods – 1937-39, 1946-47 and 1950-53 before the establishment of the Southern Area League.

California opened in 1933 and ran continuously for the rest of the decade, also staging a meeting in 1940. Post-war resumption came in 1948 and racing continued on an open licence basis until the inception of the Southern Area League.

Brafield Stadium, located in the South Northamptonshire countryside close to the village of Brafield-on-the-Green staged midget car racing in 1949 and the track was used for training in 1951. By 1953 former Norwich rider Paddy Mills (real name Horace Burke) had established a speedway training school at Brafield, transferring his activities from nearby Earls Barton, and the venue was a natural for the new Southern Area League.

Matchams Park, Ringwood, can lay claim to have produced one of the brightest stars of British speedway, Brian Crutcher,. Brian's meteoric rise to fame pre-dated the establishment of the Southern Area League but his experiences at Ringwood provide a perfect example of what the Southern training circuits were able to achieve and his success certainly inspired many more young hopefuls who learnt their trade in the SAL.

Brian Crutcher had a family background in the sport. His father Tommy, a well-known grass track rider, had raced speedway at Ringwood in the years between the World Wars and his uncle Jack Crutcher was the man who introduced the sport to Poole in 1948 and was also involved at the New Forest circuit. Brian recalls:

> I first rode on a dirt track at Ringwood on Boxing Day 1950, when I was sixteen years old. I thought I was doing quite well until two other riders, one of whom was Jimmy Squibb, went past me like rockets. It made me think, but I kept at it and in the end didn't do too badly in speedway. The track at Matchams Park had a good surface and there were a lot of good riders racing there at the time I first got on a speedway bike. Ringwood certainly helped my career to take off.

Crutcher's natural talent was such that there was no prolonged apprenticeship at an open licence track; he progressed from complete novice to a heavy scorer and breaker of

Ringwood, situated in the New Forest within easy reach of established speedway centres at Southampton and Poole were also founder members of the Southern Area League in 1954. The pick-up used for the victory parade advertises speedway at Matchams Park.
(Barry Dowden/John Somerville Collection.)

California Poppies 1954. Standing l-r, Fred Millward (team manager), Pete Mould, Jim Gleed, Gil Goldfinch, Fred Babcock, Ron Webb, George Griffin (Hon Sec California Motorcycle Club). Kneeling, l-r, Bob Andrews and George Baker. On machine is Ron Sharp. (Alf Weedon/John Somerville Collection.)

track records in a matter of eighteen months at the most. His modest comments do scant justice to his record. Born in Parkstone, Dorset, his obvious natural talent shone through to such an extent during his sessions at Ringwood that several clubs, including Division One Harringay, began to compete for his signature on a contract.

Poole, at that stage in Division Three, won the race and Brian made his debut at Wimborne Road on 24 April 1951. The occasion was a subsidiary competition, the Festival of Britain Trophy, named after the year-long event held on the South Bank in London. Meetings were run with ten man teams over 20 heats, the perfect opportunity for a team to blood young talent.

Few riders can ever have grasped such an opportunity quite as well as Crutcher, especially one who had first ridden a speedway bike just four months earlier. He took three rides and won them all, in one heat coming within 0.6 second of the existing Wimborne Road track record, as Poole defeated Exeter by 70 points to 50. The other maximum man in the Pirates' scorechart was Ken Middleditch, no stranger himself to Ringwood, with 18 points from six rides.

Brian was soon established in the Poole side and his record for the rest of the 1951 season was phenomenal. He scored 17 maximums and broke the track record on three separate occasions, as Poole won the Division Three title. The 1952 season continued his triumphant progress, which helped Poole win the Division Two championship at the first attempt. Brian scored 541 points including 19 maximums at an average of 9.41 points a match and reached the World Championship Final at Wembley. He was a world-class superstar at the age of eighteen.

The question of promotion to the National League Division One in the early 1950s, before the collapse of the London 'big five' domination, was a sensitive issue. The sport's authorities justified the denial of promotion to clubs like Poole, Norwich and Bristol on the grounds that their crowd levels and the spectator capacity of their stadiums were insufficient to make a place at the sport's top table viable.

Brian Crutcher had little choice but to look for a move, if his career was to maintain its momentum. He had already gained international honours for England and regular competition against the top men in the game was necessary if he was to completely fulfil his potential. In the end, he went right to the top, signing for Wembley for a reputed transfer fee of £2500. He remained at the Empire Stadium for three seasons, until Wembley

Alby Golden of Ringwood, later to make a name with Southampton and Newport, won the first Southern Area League Riders' Championship final at Rye House in 1954, in a run-off with Turfs' team-mate Ernie Lessiter. (Doug Booth/John Somerville Collection.)

closed, and then moved back to the South Coast to join Southampton for three more seasons in speedway. His honours included three more World Final appearances, with Brian runner-up to Ronnie Moore in 1954, and victory in the prestigious London Riders Championship in 1956.

Quite a few riders, for one reason or another, had enjoyed successful but relatively brief careers. Not many however have achieved so much at an age when many hopeful riders are hardly out of the junior stage. Brian says:

> I retired in May 1960, at Oxford. I was just twenty-five years old. I had worked in a couple of jobs after leaving school but from the time I joined Poole to the present day I never worked for anyone again. I established my own business in the motor trade and that has kept me occupied ever since.

The first detailed mentions of what was to become the SAL appeared in the speedway media in the weeks leading up to the 1954 season. In the middle of March however, the working title of the new competition was still the Metropolitan League, a name that was to resurface for a short-lived competition involving clubs outside the main league structures in 1964.

Speedway News reported that the six teams who were to eventually start the season had applied for racing licences and paid the necessary fees. Home meetings were planned to take place fortnightly on Sunday afternoons, with the exception of Aldershot where Saturday evening racing would be staged. The league would be semi-professional, using novices to make up the teams, and the prize money was expected to be seven shillings and sixpence (thirty seven and a half pence in decimal coinage), with a minimum guarantee that each riding taking part in a meeting would receive at least thirty shillings (one pound fifty pence in modern currency).

The *News* coupled the announcement about the fledgling competition with a statement that a similar sort of idea was taking place in the North, a proposal which sadly came to nothing. The creation of the SAL/Metropolitan League was given a warm welcome by *News* editor Len Went, although his story only merited a very small headline. Went said:

> If these new leagues get cracking on a sound footing and things go with a swing, it will undoubtedly prove a great boon to speedway. Top clubs are crying out for new faces and personalities – training track leagues could be the sport's salvation.

The bold headlines in the speedway press as the 1954 season began were concerned with a likely strike by riders in Division Two, over a move by promoters to impose a cut in prize money and travel expenses. The threat was eventually lifted but coverage in the mainstream press was unwelcome to a sport already facing difficulties.

The Metropolitan League/SAL was launched over a period of a month. Aldershot staged the first league meeting, beating Eastbourne 55-29 at Tongham on Saturday 17 April. Just over a week later California and Eastbourne both introduced the new competition to their fans, with both sides suffering home defeats. California lost by 38 points to 45 to Ringwood and on the same day Eastbourne were beaten by Rye House, by 49 points to 34.

There was double action too on Sunday 2 May, when Rye House beat California 47-37 and Brafield beat Eastbourne by 50-33. The final track to present racing in the new league was Ringwood, which opened on Sunday 16 May, with a 51-33 victory for the Turfs over visitors Eastbourne.

The declared aim of running the league with novices was fairly well adhered to, although there were one or two riders with National League or Southern League experience in earlier years. Ron Burnett, who had ridden in most of Aldershot's Southern League matches in 1952, was the Shots' top scorer in their home league debut win over Eastbourne, with a 12 point maximum, whilst in the same match Norman Street, who had topped St Austell's averages in the Southern section in 1952, scoring more than 250 points, was the Eagles leading scorer .

Street scored a 12 point maximum for Eastbourne in the Eagles first home league match on 25 April, but after a few more good scores was out of the Arlington line-up until the early autumn.

The league's first season featured many riders who were to win league and individual honours with SAL teams and then go on to build successful careers in the National League, the Provincial League and in some instances well into the British League in the later 1960s.

Alby Golden and Merv Hanham of Ringwood and later Southampton, Eric Hockaday and Tommy Sweetman, initially with Aldershot in 1954, Vic Ridgeon and Jimmy Heard of Rye House, and Bob Andrews, Gil Goldfinch, Ross Gilbertson and Ron Sharp of California are just a few among many examples.

Speedway being speedway, the successful launch of the new competition had not been without controversy, particularly over its name. The wrangling was sternly criticised by leading speedway journalist of the period Howard Jacobi, whose Midlands beat included Brafield. Jacobi wrote in the *Speedway News* edition of 12 May 1954, when the competition was well under way:

> The problem of finding a name for the Novice Amateur League, Metropolitan League, or what have you, seems to be causing quite a bit of a stir. I understand the Control Board is a little peeved that the new league went ahead with their 'Metropolitan' nomenclature without receiving permission, and I also understand that not all of the tracks concerned were in favour of that title.
>
> Not surprising, for the league contains tracks very far removed from the Metropolitan area. It is most unfortunate that the name of the league will have to be changed in mid-stream, more especially when the national daily newspapers have been giving match results under the heading 'Metropolitan League'.
>
> It seems to be one of those pieces of organised chaos particularly associated with speedway – and not calculated to make sports editors love us any better.

Jacobi also wrote that Coventry promoter Charles Ochilree had, 'characteristically', been the only outside official to attend Brafield's opening meeting to find out for himself what the new league was all about. Ochiltree's verdict was that the amateurs could not live without the help and assistance of their bigger brethren. Jacobi added:

In other words, if these newcomers to league racing are seen as opposition, then they will undoubtedly be crushed. If they play their promised role as training tracks, which must directly help the full-time tracks, then they are likely to receive every assistance and should survive.

The implied threat in Jacobi's words about the fate of the new league should it be seen as opposition to the National League has echoes of what had happened to rider Reg Duval's 1957 revival of Liverpool which failed, Duval claimed, due to obstacles placed in his way by certain promoters in the sport's top tier.

When the dust cleared the title of Southern Area League became official. *Speedway News* gave the competition its blessing and started a weekly column devoted to SAL results, news and views. The columnist was not afraid to express opinions. Norman Street, mentioned earlier as a top man in professional league racing with St Austell, made it into the column after scoring a maximum (mentioned earlier in this chapter). The *Speedway News* column made it clear that in the opinion of the writer a rider of Street's experience and stature 'together with several others should not be in this sphere of racing'. It was an argument that was to resurface several years later during the first season of the Provincial League.

Brafield Flying Foxes', based in the Northamptonshire countryside, were the northernmost track in the SAL. This is the 1955 line-up: Standing, l-r, Vic Hall, Alan Pearce, Brian Meredith, Dave Hankins, Colin Gooddy. Front, kneeling: Brian Miller, Fran Greasley. Neil Roberts on machine. (Peter Morrish/John Somerville Collection.)

By early June 1954 the SAL's promising newcomers were starting to attract the attention of National League tracks. The magazine column was full of praise for twenty-year-old Jack (Jimmy) Heard, a Plaistow boy who after just six weeks in the sport and tutoring by former Australian test star Dick Case, had scored a maximum for Rye House against Brafield. Another Rye House rider, Vic Ridgeon, had been invited to Plymouth for a trial but his trip had not been a great success. He put this down to having driven to Devon immediately after finishing work on a night shift and being dog-tired on arrival!

By the middle of July the only SAL team without a win was Eastbourne, one of the competition's most well established venues. *Speedway News* put this down to the fact that the Arlington side appeared to be 'the only REAL novice combination in the SAL'.

Aldershot, at one time leading the league table, were to provide the first unpleasant shock for the Southern Area League. Proving that it never pays to count chickens in speedway, the SAL columnist in the *News* ended his column in mid-June by stating that crowds in the league were 'up, everywhere'. A fortnight later and the Shots were out. The writer was distraught, saying:

Only a couple of weeks ago we stressed that the Southern Area League was a strong and healthy child. The ink was hardly dry before all that was virtually knocked on the head. Aldershot had closed, and the team's record had been deleted from the league tables.

On the basis that it never rains but it pours, there were moves in Northamptonshire to obtain an injunction to prevent Brafield from racing on a Sunday, with rumours circulating that Paddy Mills intended to move the Flying Foxes team to Long Eaton, should the legal action succeed.

The initial racing format of the SAL was based on each track racing the other teams four times in total, twice at home and twice away, making a total of 20 matches. After

Aldershot's withdrawal their record was expunged from the league table and Rye House became the first title holders with ten wins and 20 points from the 16 matches that counted. California, Ringwood and Brafield all finished on 18 points, two fewer than Rye House. The Poppies took the runners-up spot on the basis of having scored more race points and had the side been successful against the Turfs in that first home match that same bumper haul of race points would have been sufficient to edge Rye House out of first place.

California historian Bryan Horsnell argues convincingly in his excellent publication *California Speedway – The Southern Area League Years of the Poppies 1954-57* that his side's defeat by 45-33 to Ringwood in their first SAL home match cost them the title. As the season progressed California had strengthened their team considerably, introducing Jim Gleed, future World Finalist Bob Andrews, and Peter Mould into the team. Bryan Horsnell adds:

> With Tommy Sweetman and Eric Hockday, who were recruited following the closure of Aldershot it was generally accepted that the Poppies were the strongest team in the Southern Area League.

Outside the top four Eastbourne, despite the track's long history, experienced a truly torrid season. The league table shows them with three wins and six points, but gives a slightly false impression. The Eagles had to wait until the middle of August for their first win of the season, by the narrow margin of 41-37 against Brafield.

In 1955 Ringwood followed the example set by Aldershot in the SAL's first campaign, withdrawing in mid-season. Turfs' rider Ken Middleditch, later of Poole and Swindon, leads Johnny Thomson, who died following a track crash at Poole. (Barry Dowden/John Somerville Collection.)

Eastbourne actually raced only 15 matches, with double points being awarded for their second home fixture against the Flying Foxes. The result duly registered as two wins in the final league table. The Eagles, who never made their second scheduled trip of the season to Northamptonshire, officially finished with three wins and six points, a very long way behind everyone else. Aldershot, ironically in view of their mid-season closure, blamed on poor crowds, had enjoyed a reasonably good season, winning five of the ten matches they raced

The Southern Area League had its major individual event in the shape of the SAL Riders Championship, staged at Rye House on Sunday 3 October and won by Alby Golden of Ringwood. Golden beat Ernie Lessiter, also of the Turfs, in a run-off after both men had scored 14 points in the meeting. Vic Ridgeon of Rye House was third.

The five teams that finished the SAL's inaugural season lined up again for the 1955 campaign although once again the new league's record was marred by a mid-season withdrawal, this time of Ringwood. Rye House were champions again, winning ten of their twelve matches to give them a clear six point margin over runners-up California, who had seven league victories. Brafield were third, winning six, whilst Eastbourne were again wooden spoonists, with just one victory to their credit. Ringwood, at the time of withdrawal, had won two of their eight SAL fixtures.

At the start of the SAL's first season the fans at each track had been able to anticipate ten home league matches, a figure reduced to eight by the withdrawal of Aldershot. For 1955, with one less track operating, the scheduled home league clashes were down to eight, further reduced to six when Ringwood quit. A more or less full season was maintained by the staging of individual meetings and challenge matches and by the inclusion in the fixture list of qualifying rounds at Rye House, Eastbourne and California for the SAL Riders' Championship, which in 1954 had seen riders nominated for the final by their clubs.

The final, at Hoddesdon on Sunday 25 September, was won by Rye House's rapidly rising young star Mike Broadbank. The future 'Red Devil', who won the nickname for the red leathers he adopted in an era when speedway riders were still truly Men in Black, recorded a 15 point maximum to lift the trophy. Added to the 14 he had notched up in his qualifying round, this meant that he had dropped only a single point in the competition.

There was an increased accent all round on really meaningful individual competition to add to the customary Easter and Whitsun trophies in the SAL in 1955, with the introduction of the Silver Sash match race title. The new innovation, which proved extremely popular, began at Brafield on Sunday 10 April, when the Flying Foxes defeated Ringwood Turfs 50-30 in a league fixture.

The individual top scorers from each side qualified to ride for the Sash and on this first occasion Brafield's Eric Croft took the honours by defeating Merv Hannam of the Turfs. The rules of the competition dictated that the holder was required to defend his title against the highest scorer of the opposing team in Brafield's next league match. This was against Rye House and Croft held on to the Sash by beating Mike Broadbank. Croft's winning run came to an end next time out when he lost the title to Pete Mould of California.

The record number of successful defences of the Sash during the 1955 season was four, by Vic Hall of Brafield, who only relinquished it when he was injured and unable to defend his title. Colin Gooddy, again of Brafield, won the season's last Sash contest against Bob Bunney of Eastbourne.

In the league Mike Broadbank was the highest scorer, with 113 points from his twelve matches for Rye House. Vic Hall was Brafield's top man with 98 points from just 10 matches, with Pete Mould of California heading the Poppies score chart with 82 points from 12 matches. At Eastbourne the top scorer, his rather meagre haul reflecting the Eagles lack of success, was Wally Wilson, with 46 points from eight matches.

During the winter of 1955-56 the number of guaranteed starters for the Southern Area League fell to just three tracks, with the withdrawal of Brafield. This was obviously not a feasible proposition but the remaining promoters of Rye House, Eastbourne and California got together to form a nomadic side, aptly called Southern Rovers. The Rovers were homeless, riding their 'home' fixtures at California, Eastbourne and Rye House and at a completely neutral venue, the Abbey Stadium home of National League Division Two side Swindon.

The four-team format allowed each club to race twelve matches in 1956. Rye House completed a hat trick of victories and Eastbourne, the league's whipping boys in '54 and '55, improved substantially and finished second. Southern Rovers were third and California occupied the bottom spot. The SAL Riders' Championship was won by Leo McAuliffe of Eastbourne and the holders of the Silver Sash during the season were Gil Goldfinch (California), Vic Ridgeon (with six victories before relinquishing the sash to Leo McAuliffe) and then Jim Gleed, Jim Heard and, once again, re-capturing the title in the last match of the season, Vic Ridgeon.

Perhaps the greatest highlight of the 1956 season was the progression of two riders from the Southern Area League to the heights of the National League Division One, swapping the modest stadia of the SAL for a home base at Wembley's Empire Stadium.

Mike Broadbank's high scoring during 1955 had attracted the notice of Wembley, who were quick to sign him for 1956. Mike was in the Wembley team from the start of the season and was subsequently joined by young Australian Ray Cresp, whose rise up the ranks was even more meteoric. Cresp made his debut for Eastbourne at California on 22 April and raised eyebrows immediately by scoring a paid maximum from four rides at reserve.

Cresp rode just three matches for the Eagles in the SAL, scoring 11 points in his second and a full maximum in his third, enough to earn the call to Wembley. He scored six points from two rides in a second half junior match against Wimbledon on 21 May and was then promoted to the full Lions team for the next home match against Birmingham, when he scored paid eight points.

Cresp and Broadbank were fixtures in the Wembley side for the rest of the 1956 season. Cresp finished with 85 league points from 18 matches whilst Broadbank scored 81 from 23 appearances. Both men fully justified the increasing interest shown by the big clubs in Southern Area League talent. Cresp was born in Melbourne, Australia, but Broadbank was a Hoddesdon man, born and bred. He worked at Rye House Stadium as a youngster, eventually making the transition to the track to launch a stellar career.

Wembley closed at the end of the 1956 season and Mike Broadbank then began a fifteen-year-career with Swindon, making 560 appearances for the Robins and scoring more than 4200 points. His team honours included winning the SAL with Rye House in 1955, the National League with Swindon in 1957 and the British League, again with the Wiltshire club, in 1967. Individual successes included five appearances in World Finals (plus two as reserve), many international appearances for his country and the London Riders Championship.

Cresp won four test caps for Australia and also made six appearances for the rather loosely titled Great Britain team. He was a World Finalist in 1961 and a British finalist the

The line-up for the 1955 Southern Area League Riders' Championship Final. Back row, l-r, Mike Broadbank, Dave Slater, Merv Hannam, Jimmy Heard, Gil Goldfinch, Bob Anderson, Tom Reader, Ross Gilbertson, Gerry King, Bob Bunney. Front row kneeling, l-r, Colin Gooddy, Tommy Sweetman, Eric Hockaday, Stan Bedford, Peter Mould, Vic Ridgeon, Brian Meredith. (Peter Morrish/John Somerville Collection.)

same year, and rode for Oxford, Ipswich, Poole and Norwich in the National League, St Austell in the Provincial League, West Ham in the final season of the National League and Long Eaton in the British League.

Mike Broadbank also established an Australian connection, when in 1963 he won the Australian Championship in Rockhampton, Queensland, pushing local rider Keith Gurtner into second place. The third spot was taken by a rider who had failed to match the exploits of Broadbank and Cresp in the Southern Area League but went on to become one of the sport's biggest names of all time – Ivan Mauger. Broadbank's success was the last time the Australian title was won by an English rider.

After his marathon stint at Swindon, Broadbank became one of speedway's nomads, racing for eight more teams until finally retiring in 1977 at the age of forty-three. During his twenty-two-year-career in speedway he never forgot his roots at Rye House, maintaining an association that included stints as training school instructor, track constructor and promoter. At one stage the Rye House team's nickname, the Roosters at the start of the track's Southern Area League career, was changed to the Red Devils in honour of their greatest track hero.

During the 1956 season several men from the Southern Area League who were to build successful careers at the top level of speedway started to take off. The in-depth strength possessed at the start of that season by London's sole-surviving teams Wimbledon and Wembley, who finished first and second respectively in the National League Division One allowed them to take a chance of young riders from the Southern Area League.

Few if any progressions from the SAL to Division One were to prove as rapid and successful as the experiences enjoyed by Broadbank and Cresp. But in 1956 Gil Goldfinch and Bob Andrews made more than 30 appearances between them in a Wimbledon team which at the end of the campaign boasted three of the leading scorers in the division in Barry Briggs, Ronnie Moore and Peter Moore. In addition to Broadbank and Cresp, Merv Hannam rode in 13 matches for the Lions and Tommy Sweetman (Dons) and Bobby Croombs (Wembley) both made Division One debuts.

The top three teams in Division Two of the National League in 1956 all included riders nurtured in the SAL. Champions Swindon had three SAL men in Ernie Lessiter, Albert Sparrey and Glyn Chandler, runners-up Southampton tracked Alby Golden (who had already made the step up for 1955) and Ron Sharp, whilst third placed Rayleigh tracked Eric Ebbs, Pete Mould and Fred Greenwell, the latter rider a rare example of a North Country junior trying his luck in the South.

Another leading light in the SAL, Eric Hockaday, won a place at Coventry in 1956, although he insists to this day that this was not entirely down to his promise as a rider. Eric explains:

> I lived at the time close to Heathrow Airport. Charles Ochiltree had signed the Swedish rider Per Olaf Soderman and it was convenient for the CO to have someone to act as his chauffeur from the airport to Brandon and back again.

The 1957 Southern Area League is one of those (not uncommon) areas of speedway where the aspiring historian needs to tread carefully. The four teams contesting the league in its fourth season of existence comprised ever-presents Rye House and Eastbourne, a returning venue in the form of Aldershot and a new venue, new that is as far as the SAL was concerned.

The trap for the unwary aspiring historian lies in the fact that two of the nicknames from the previous season were in use again, but applied to different teams. California withdrew from the competition but the track's management transferred to returning Aldershot , and took with them both the core of the team and the nickname, operating for the new campaign as Aldershot Poppies.

There was a major change in store too for the wandering Southern Rovers, who for 1957 were to be based at The Weir Stadium, Rayleigh and would race as Rayleigh Rovers. The Weir would effectively see a track share as Rayleigh Rockets, in existence since 1948 and runners-up in the 1956 National League Division Two, had become members of the newly merged one big National League.

It meant a full programme for Rayleigh fans, with 12 National League home fixtures for the Rockets together with matches in the Britannia Shield and challenge matches, plus the six league fixtures and the Final of the Southern Area League Riders Championship for the SAL men. Two of Rayleigh's National League fixtures were actually raced at the end of the season at Wimborne Road, Poole, with the team billed as the Rayleigh Pirates; Poole were operating on an open licence in 1957.

For the first time in the history of the SAL the championship trophy went elsewhere than Rye House Stadium. In fact the triple-champions of 1954-56 finished rock bottom of the league.

Working out the detailed reasons for Rye House's decline in 1957 is not a simple task given the time gap of more than sixty years. Over the first three seasons of the SAL the competition had been reasonably closely contested, with the notable exception in 1954 and 1955 of Eastbourne, when the Eagles recorded only four league victories from a total of 28 matches.

With only three declared starters for the SAL in 1956, the other promoters formed a nomadic side, Southern Rovers. Pictured, l-r standing, are: Tony Eadon, Bert Little, Colin Gooddy, Eric Hockaday, Dave Hankins, Les King (manager). Front row kneeling, Eric Eadon (left) and Brian Meredith. Neil Roberts on machine. (John Somerville Collection.)

Conversation piece. Rye House team mates Al Sparrey (centre) and Vic Ridgeon listen attentively to Tommy Sweetman of California. Rye House won their third successive SAL title in 1956 whilst Vic Ridgeon ended the season in possession of the league's Silver Sash. (Peter Morrish/John Somerville Collection.)

A cigarette break for rising Rye House star Brian Brett, a protégé of Mike Broadbank in 1956. Brett qualified for the SAL Riders' Chamionship final on his home track, scoring a creditable eight points. (Peter Morrish/John Somerville Collection.)

There was no huge gap between top and bottom in 1957. Champions Rayleigh Rovers finished with 16 points, four clear of runners-up Eastbourne but in the lower half of the table Aldershot and Rye House both had five wins apiece from their 12 matches, with the Shots avoiding bottom spot thanks to a superior race points position.

The Roosters were strong enough on paper, with Vic Ridgeon, Brian Brett, Bobby Croombs, Al Sparrey and Gerry King and in June recorded a crushing 66-17 victory over an Eastbourne side apparently much improved from the past two campaigns. Perhaps the highlight of the season for the former triple champions came at The Weir Stadium, Rayleigh in June when the Roosters inflicted a 44-40 home defeat on the Rovers, their successors as SAL champions.

The other side of the coin was a 60-23 defeat for the Roosters at Aldershot in September. Rye House on that day showed one or two changes from the team from earlier in the season, including two teenagers who were to go on to make a mark in the sport.

Not on this occasion though. Colin Pratt and a young New Zealander called Ivan Mauger scored but a single point between them, with Mauger suffering engine failure in two races and Pratt being excluded in his first ride!

The 1957 Southern Area League Riders' Championship was won for a second successive year by Leo McAuliffe, this time wearing the colours of Rayleigh rather than Eastbourne, his club side at the time of his earlier title success. The competition's Silver Sash winners during the season were Frank Bettis (four victories during the campaign), Pete Mould, Vic Hall and Leo McAuliffe (three late victories and the holder at the end of the season)

There was no Southern Area League in 1958, although there still existed what can be called the SAL circuit. Rye House and Eastbourne continued in much the same vein as they had operated before the Sunday league was created, although the Hoddesdon track had fewer meetings than usual. Aldershot had a short season, racing just two fixtures at home and one away at Eastbourne. California staged just one meeting, the California Championship, won by Eric Hockaday, who enjoyed a full season in the National League at Coventry, racing in 18 matches fixtures, averaging nearly four points a match.

Taking a snapshot of the overall picture in the South of England in 1957/58, the more favourable financial climate which had encouraged Reg Duval to take a chance at Liverpool in 1957 also set the scene for a mini-revival in the South West of England.

Exeter had resigned from National League Division Two after finishing bottom of the section in 1955. The County Ground was quiet in 1956 but former Falcons favourite Jack Geran and veteran Geoff Pymar re-opened the track at the end of July 1957 for a short run of eight meetings, challenge matches and individual events using mainly National League riders, giving the Devon fans a chance to see the likes of Ove Fundin, Brian Crutcher, Peter Craven and Aub Lawson. For the challenge matches, against Norwich, Oxford, Southampton and Swindon the Exeter line-up included former Falcons Geran and Neil Street, Bob and Cyril Roger and Francis Cann. An additional attraction was an England v Overseas match, with the Overseas team winning 50-46.

Exeter operated on an Open Licence again in 1958, staging six meetings, again with a majority of the riders coming from the National League, including Split Waterman, who appeared for Southampton in a challenge match. One notable challenge match brought the eventual National League champions, Wimbledon, to the County Ground and and 1957 World Champion Barry Briggs (who was to repeat his triumph in '58) thrilled the West Country fans with a faultless 18 point maximum. The consolation for the Exeter supporters was the Falcons' 51-45 match victory over the Dons.

Further to the south-west St Austell, last seen in league racing in 1953, staged a short season in 1958 during the peak holiday period. The weather was unkind, with only four meetings completed, two being rained off and one abandoned. Again, the fixtures mostly provided bookings for established National League men, including Ronnie Moore, Peter Craven and Barry Briggs, although there were also chances for West Country-based Francis Cann, Chris Julian, Chris Blewett and SAL man Brian Brett.

There had been some very limited speedway action elsewhere in London in the 1950s, continuing until 1958. White City Stadium in West London, which had last staged the sport seriously in 1928, ran a series of Composite events from 1953 to 1958 inclusive. These consisted of match races, run over two heats and a final, featuring some of the biggest, mostly London-based names in speedway.

Exeter 1957, when riders Jack Geran and Geoff Pymar promoted open licence meetings following the abolition of entertainment tax. Pictured, back row, l-r, are Pymar (co-promoter), Cliff Cox, unknown, Cyril Roger, Geran (co-promoter), unknown, Neil Street. Kneeling, front, -l-r, Trevor Redmond, Francis Cann, Glyn Chandler. (John Somerville Collection.)

Yarmouth, Southern Area League 1959. Standing, l-r, Tony Childs, Ivor Brown, Johnny Fitzpatrick, John Debbage, Ken Last, Dave Hankins, Ted Courtnell (promoter). Al Sparrey on machine. (John Somerville Collection.)

Riders who took part over the years included Jack Young, Bill Kitchen, Freddie Williams, and Ronnie Moore.

In 1955 the riders were stated to have used Vespa scooters, very fashionable in the era, rather than speedway machines!

Harringay, which had closed early in 1954 and fully embraced stock car racing, staged a Cavalcade of Speed event at the end of November with match races between former Racers' Split Waterman, Alf Hagon, Danny Dunton and Ron How. Waterman and How won the heats and Waterman defeated How in the final.

Although there was no SAL in 1958, an attempt was made to partly fill the gap with a Junior League, consisting of teams representing Poole, Norwich, Yarmouth and Swindon. The fixtures were not completed. The first three named teams each won two matches, scoring four match points whilst Swindon managed to complete four matches, but without a single success.

The Southern Area League's fortunes revived significantly in 1959 after the blank campaign of the year before. In fact the competition, suspended in 1958 when it was impossible to field the minimum of four teams needed for a viable league, could conceivably have enjoyed the most successful campaign in its relatively brief history if all the pre-season possibilities had been realised.

It had become fairly customary each year for the final confirmation of membership of the league to be delayed until quite close to the due date for the opening meetings. In 1959 the process was even more complex than usual. Eastbourne and Rye House, the long-established tracks which had formed the hard core of the SAL since its inception, were certain to run but the identity of the other tracks took some time and negotiation to establish.

Rayleigh, which in 1957 had hosted the former Southern Rovers team and had won the league title, withdrew for 1959 and were replaced by Ipswich, which had dropped out of the National League after a disastrous campaign in 1958. The new promotion in Suffolk, headed by Australian World Finalist and Test star Aub Lawson ran a mixed season, alternating fortnightly open licence meetings using top National League riders with a new team of juniors in the SAL, sometimes (although not always) being billed as the Foxhall Heath Witches.

A little farther up the East coast in Norfolk Yarmouth signed up for a place in the 1959 SAL. The Bloaters had last run as a league club in 1953 but re-opened on an open licence for 1957-58. As a holiday resort the track ran only during the peak holiday weeks from late June/early July to the beginning of September

With Eastbourne, Rye House, Ipswich/Foxhall and Yarmouth as certain starters, the SAL had sufficient teams to operate in 1959. Behind the scenes however stock car driver and promoter Chez Chesson was negotiating to open a track at Sittingbourne in Kent (in later years a Conference League and training track at Iwade, Kent, and not to be confused with the present-day Kent team based at Central Park, Sittingbourne).

Ted Payne, team manager for Southern/Rayleigh Rovers in previous seasons, was lined up for the same job for Sittingbourne and a team had been announced including such well-known and experienced SAL riders as Ron Sharp, Brian Meredith, Arthur Ashby, Dave Freeborn, Bob Thomas, Eric Eadon and Roy Pickering, followed by the signing of Southampton prospect Peter Vandenberg.

As things turned out, Sittingbourne did not, on this occasion, materialise for Southern Area League speedway and the team put together by Chesson and Payne looked like competing as Southern Rovers in the 1959 competition (nomadic or based somewhere else?). Historian and contributor to the *Speedway Researcher* website Keith Corns has made a close study of the run-up to the Southern Area League's 1959 campaign and explains:

> It appears that the Southern Rovers team would have been based at Sittingbourne or at Lydden Hill in Kent, which was a well-known grass track (and later stock car) circuit and was owned by Chesson. Although it became clear at an early date that this was not possible, the name Southern Rovers continued to be used pending the result of negotiations by Ted Payne to base operations at Tongham Stadium, Aldershot.

> My guess is that if Aldershot had not materialised the choice for Payne would have lain between pulling out of the league or reverting to the old Rovers' nomadic status, riding matches on the tracks of the other SAL teams.

Yarmouth also re-opened for 1957 and 1958 on an open licence, before joining the SAL for 1959. The Norfolk track operated during the peak holiday weeks of the season and the advertising van pictured toured the seafront in a bid to attract holidaymakers. (John Somerville Collection.)

Chiswick Nomads 1958.
Standing, l-r, Arthur
Ashby, Mike
Chamberlain,Tom
Deacon, Clive Hitch,
Dennis Denton
(mechanic), Terry
Denton (mechanic).
Front, l-r, Malcolm
Reading, Ted Payne
(secretary and founder
on bike), Bob Thomas.
(John Somerville
Collection.)

Aldershot's application for a licence was initially rejected by the Control Board but Ted Payne appealed and managed to get the decision reversed.

When SAL racing did get underway, one major difference between what was to prove the league's final season and the campaigns that had gone before was the number of matches raced. In 1954 the fixture list had envisaged ten home and ten away matches per side, a figure reduced by the withdrawal of Aldershot. In 1955 there should have been 16 matches in total, reduced to 12 when Ringwood pulled out, whilst in 1956 and 1957, with four starters and no withdrawals, each side raced 12 matches.

In 1959, when the number of clubs increased, initially at least, to six, the league's management committee decided that each team should ride one match at home and one away against their opponents, rather than the two at home and two away formula which had existed in the previous SAL seasons.

Some statistical summaries do not acknowledge the Southern Rovers involvement in the 1959 SAL at all. But the *Speedway Researcher* website carries the details of two matches for the nomadic club that year, one a challenge and one a league fixture. Both matches were at Eastbourne and both ended in home victories, by 46-26 in the challenge match on Sunday 3 May and by 38-34 in the SAL fixture on 31 May.

The programme for the second match at Eastbourne involving Chesson and Payne's team referred to 'Kent' rather than 'Southern Rovers', presumably because hopes were still alive at that stage that the side would find a home at either Sittingbourne or Lydden Hill.

The team line-ups for both the challenge match and the SAL fixture at Arlington included the riders Chesson and Payne had recruited earlier. Most of these managed to secure rides for other SAL sides after the Rovers' withdrawal; Vandenberg for Southampton in the National Reserve League and Aldershot, Eadon, Pickering and Edwards (Aldershot) whilst Bob Thomas made appearances for Ipswich, the Shots and Eastbourne.

When Aldershot finally got the go-ahead to run in the SAL the result of the league match at Arlington was credited to the Shots' record in the league table.

With the identity of the league's competitors at last sorted out, fans could look forward to the season's racing. There was particular satisfaction at Ipswich, where for some time in the previous winter it appeared that there would be no speedway at Foxhall in 1959. The Witches had finished rock bottom of the National League in 1958, with just one win from 18 matches and attendances had plummeted.

The saviours of the Suffolk track were enthusiast Harold Soanes and the legendary Australian Test star and ten times World Finalist Aub Lawson, who first came to England in 1939, riding for Division One Wembley and Division Two Middlesbrough and qualifying for the September World Final which was cancelled due to the outbreak of World War Two. Aub's post-war career, between 1947 and 1960, was spent with just two clubs, West Ham and, for eight seasons between 1953 and 1960, with Norwich.

Fearing for the future of Ipswich, Soanes wrote to his friend Lawson in Perth, West Australia, where Aub was promoting and riding at Claremont, in Perth. Lawson later explained:

> Whilst I was ten thousand miles away Herbert wrote to say there was to be no speedway at Ipswich and asked if I could do something to prevent such a calamity. My contract at Claremont prevented me from returning to England in time to stop the Ipswich team being disbanded. We decided to go ahead at Foxhall anyway, with me as managing director and we staged top class racing every second Thursday with the world's best riders and entered a team of juniors in the Southern Area League.

Yarmouth had last run as a league club in 1953 but re-opened on an open licence for 1957-58. In their open licence seasons Yarmouth had mainly used National League men, providing much needed additional bookings. Aldershot, after enjoying a full season in the Southern Area League in 1957, managed only three recorded open licence meetings in '58, but returned for the '59 SAL campaign, welcoming Eric Hockaday back to the competition after his National League spell at Coventry.

Competition was fairly close in the SAL in 1959, with no whipping boys as had occurred in early seasons. Eastbourne, who had endured difficult times in the early league campaigns, finishing bottom of the table in 1954 and 1955 before climbing to second spot in '56 and '57, made it to the top in the league's final year, with a two point margin over Yarmouth. Aldershot were third with eight points, whilst Rye House, triple champions in the 1954-56 period, squeezed above bottom placed Ipswich on race points.

In January 1959 *Speedway Star* reported that a party of Dutch riders hoped to spend a week racing in Britain, in team events on SAL tracks against a 'Junior England' side. The magazine speculated that as the Dutch riders who would make up the party were likely to be 'well above' SAL standards, it would be necessary for 'Junior England' to use National League second strings to boost their side. In the event, the tour did not materialise.

The main individual honours for the final SAL season went to Dave Hankins of Yarmouth. In the season that saw his National League debut for Leicester Hunters and regular rides in the National Reserve League, he limbered up by lifting the Bosch Trophy at Yarmouth and the Suffolk Junior Championship at Ipswich – the runner-up was the veteran Wal Morton, born in 1910, who had first ridden speedway in 1933!

Hankins then crowned his season by winning the SAL Riders' Championship final with a 15-point maximum at Foxhall Heath, Ipswich, on 26 September 1959, from Derek Timms (13 points) and Ivor Brown (12). He was also the man in possession of the Silver Sash at the end of the season. Colin Goody of Eastbourne had held the Sash for much of the season, recording four victories but met his match in August at Arlington. It was a bad afternoon for the local fans as Eastbourne lost at home to the Bloaters and Hankins outpaced Goody in the match race.

Dave Hankins was very much a graduate of the Southern Area League. When the competition was founded in 1954 he joined Brafield with fellow Leicester juniors Vic Hall and Doug Jackson. When Brafield closed at the end of 1955 he made a fleeting appearance

Rye House 1959. The three-times Southern Area League champions had a poor season by their high standards, finishing next to bottom – an improvement on their wooden spoon in 1957. Pictured, standing l-r, Ronnie Rolfe, Stan Stevens, Bill Wainwright, Fred Peachey (manager), Pete Sampson, Ernie Baker, Clive Hitch Bobby Croombs. Tommy Sweetman on the machine. (Peter Morrish/John Somerville Collection.)

the following season for Southern Rovers and then spent much of the 1956 season on loan at Norwich, making his senior debut in a Britannia Shield match. Although soon returned to second halves, he persevered and his successes in 1959 were just reward.

A winter trip to Australia followed and Dave, based in Perth, raced for the Lions against the Kangaroos in an unofficial three match series, scoring seven points overall. When he returned to Leicester for the 1960 season he was offered a full contract and he scored solidly in his first full senior season. With the 1961 season just seven weeks old he contracted pneumonia and pleurisy. And it was July before he was able to resume racing but he broke a thigh in a World Championship qualifying round at New Cross, which effectively cut short a promising career.

The 1959 season was not quite the end of the road for the Southern Area League. In 1960 men who had learnt their trade in the competition were nominated for what was to prove the last SAL Riders' Championship Final, held at Eastbourne on 25 September. Ross Gilbertson, who had ridden for the Arlington Eagles in the last year of the SAL took the title with a 15 point maximum, ahead of Stan Stevens and Ken Adams.

In 1963 there was speculation in the speedway media about the formation of a new Southern Area League. This eventually materialised in 1964 and, with a neat turn of the circle, it was named the Metropolitan League – the original title proposed for the SAL in 1954.

Before turning attention to the rapidly increasing level of speedway activity *outside* the National and Southern Area Leagues at the end of the decade of the 1950s, it is worth pausing to consider the links between the SAL and its tracks in the period 1957-58 and one of the greatest (some would say THE greatest) speedway riders of all times – Ivan Mauger.

Chapter 4

IVAN MAUGER AND THE SOUTHERN AREA LEAGUE

Ivan: Disillusionment on first trip to the UK

ONLY a select band of men can be found today whose active association with speedway racing dates back over eight decades. As rider, promoter and administrator Reg Fearman has been present at many of the occasions that, with hindsight, can be seen as unusually significant in the history of the sport – some joyful, some tragic and one at least that historians will always see as initiating a new era in speedway, in so many different ways.

The location for the latter event was Aranui Speedway in Christchurch, New Zealand. During the 1954 season Fearman had become one of many British riders to fear for his racing future. The wholesale closure of the Scottish tracks at Glasgow Ashfield, Glasgow White City and Edinburgh (Motherwell was soon to follow) had released their star men on to the transfer market. Reg recalls:

I had worked my way up at Leicester to become number two in the team rankings. First Ken McKinlay arrived at Blackbird Road and then the Hunters signed two more riders from North of the Border in Ron Phillips and Gordon McGregor. I could see the writing on the wall and to a recently-married man the thought of being out of a job was unacceptable. The management of the Western Springs track in Auckland had invited me to race there in the winter of 1954; my

Ivan Mauger with his speedway machines, at home in Christchurch NZ before his first UK trip. (Reg Fearman Collection.)

wife Joan and I decided to accept and we went to New Zealand with an open mind as to how long we would stay there.

That was how, on 8 October 1955, Reg could be found in the Aranui pits, following a 474 mile trip by road and ferry, crossing from the country's North Island to the South. It was his debut at the venue but another rider was making a much more significant bow, in the form of his first speedway race in public.

Ivan Mauger had passed his sixteenth birthday just four days earlier and had the misfortune to see his name misprinted in the programme as 'Major', but took second place in the Aranui novice event, taking home a cheque for £1 – ten shillings (50p) for his second place and ten shillings start money. He later framed the cheque and hung it on the wall of his home.

Reg Fearman has wondered on many occasions what was running through the mind that evening of a teenager who subsequently brought previously unheard of levels of sheer professionalism and determination to everything he did in speedway. Reg says in his autobiography *Both Sides of the Fence* (The History Press ISBN 978075095848):

> It was the very first race on the programme and he must have been quite nervous riding out of the pits in front of 10,000 speedway fans. But the Ivan I knew was a very determined, one could almost say, driven young man. From an early age he had made up his mind to be a speedway rider and this ambition stayed with him despite the false start to his career in England a little later in the 1950s.

Mauger's dedication led to him working at after school, weekend and holiday jobs to get the money for a speedway machine and, later, to afford the fare to England. As at all times during his career and in life after his retirement from speedway, he was supported by wife Raye. Ivan recalled in his autobiography *Ivan Mauger The Will to Win* (Nationwide Books ISBN 9780955237690):

> Everyone thought I had wealthy parents because I could afford to buy a bike before I was sixteen but for three years I never bought an ice-cream, a Coca-Cola or anything like that. After I left school I had two jobs – as did Raye – and that's how we saved enough money to come to England when we were little more than children.

The Aranui Speedway, Christchurch, programme for Ivan Mauger's speedway debut. (Reg Fearman Collection.)

Not for the first time a programme compiler misspelt Mauger's name. His first pay cheque from speedway was £1 – ten shillings for the start and ten shillings for being placed second in the Novice race at Aranui. (Reg Fearman Collection.)

CHRISTCHURCH AUTODROME ARANUI

No. 1
8th OCTOBER
1955
PROGRAMME 1/-

PROGRAMME

7.45 p.m.—NOVICE RACE   4 Laps
(Learners Only)
10/- Starting, First £1, Second 10/-

Rider	Colour	Handicap	Place
BILL BLAKE	Red	10	3rd
CYRIL LEE	White	Go	
BRUCE SAVAGE	Blue	Go	2nd
IVAN MAJOR	Gold and Black	Go	1st
ALBY JORDAN	White and Black	Go	

7.50 p.m.—RESERVES RACE   4 Laps
£1 Starting, First £3, Second £2

Rider	Colour	Handicap	Place
NOEL BARRITT	Red	Go	2nd
GEORGE TOPP	White	Go	
KEN REES	Blue	Go	1st

8 p.m. OFFICIAL OPENING

Event 1 — OPENING HANDICAP   4 Laps
£1 Starting. First, £5; Second, £3; Third, £1.

Rider	Colour	Handicap	Place
BRIAN McKEOWN	Red	60	
TOM JOHNSON	White	50	1st
MERV. HORTON	Blue	20	2nd
SYD. HARRISON	Gold and Black	10	3rd
PETER ADAIR	White and Black	Go	

The teenage Raye and Ivan Mauger. (Mauger family.)

The seventeen-year-old Mauger and his teenage wife Raye arrived at Tilbury Docks in the early spring of 1957 aboard the SS *Rangitoto*, followed the trail to South London already beaten with such success by fellow teenage Kiwis Ronnie Moore and Barry Briggs and rented a flat just around the corner from Wimbledon's Plough Lane Stadium.

Ivan introduced himself to Dons' promoter Ronnie Greene, told of his ambition to be a speedway rider but added that in the meantime, he needed a job. Greene provided the job, working at the club's Plough Lane stadium but also told him to turn up to the speedway press and practice day.

Wimbledon opened their 1957 season on Good Friday, 19 April, and Ivan was thrown into the deep end, being named as reserve in the Dons' team that faced a touring Polish national side in a challenge match. He owed his place to the fact that Wimbledon tracked an eight-man team and to the absence on the night of his hero Ronnie Moore.

Mauger's debut was not unpromising. He scored three points, plus two bonus. After coming in last in his first reserve ride, he finished third behind partner Bob Andrews in his second and then, with the Dons' ahead by such a large margin, was given an extra ride in the final heat, coming second behind team-mate Alf Hagon.

Although always on the lookout for a chance to race, Ivan was quite content to work on stadium and track maintenance, stating in his autobiography *The Will to Win*:

> I never, ever felt I was going to work for the simple reason that I just loved the atmosphere of being in Wimbledon Stadium. I cleaned the dressing rooms, the toilets, the pits and the workshop and helped on the track itself. I weeded the tulip beds and on Monday afternoons I had to cut the grass out in the centre before the speedway meeting. And not just any old cut would do for Ronnie {Greene}. It had to be mowed in one direction then the other, just like Wembley Stadium.

His second chance in the Wimbledon team came in May, when he was named as reserve in a match against Norwich in the Britannia Shield, failing to score. His third (and final) appearance in Dons' colours in 1957 was in the National League at Foxhall Heath, Ipswich, when Wimbledon beat the home team 50-46. Ivan was paid for two points after finishing in third place behind partner Gerry King.

In the second halves at Plough Lane his form was not outstanding and he often suffered engine failures. When Ronnie Greene staged a Junior Riders Championship Ivan was outpaced by the likes of Ernie Baker, Bobby Croombs, Gil Goldfinch and Brian Brett.

Mauger's performances in the Southern Area League sphere throughout 1957 were not much more encouraging. His first outing on the Sunday afternoon circuit came in an open meeting, the Whitsun Trophy, with three lap heats, at Rye House on 9 June. This brought Ivan what was probably his first race win in the UK, when he headed home Gil

The immaculately-maintained Wimbledon Stadium (sadly now demolished) where in 1957 Ivan Mauger determined to follow in the footsteps of New Zealand speedway heroes Ronnie Moore and Barry Briggs. Ivan was given a job on the groundstaff, with one of his tasks the cutting and trimming of the grass on the centre green. (John Somerville Collection.)

Goldfinch, Dave Still and Jim Chalkley in heat two. His next ride was blank but in heat 10 he came second to Jim Tebby and finished the meeting with five points.

He appeared for Rye House in an away Southern Area League match against Rayleigh Rovers at The Weir, scoring four points as the Roosters crashed 58-26 to the eventual champions.

Ivan's best performance of 1957 came on 4 August, at Eastbourne's Arlington Stadium, when he scored seven points from four rides to finish in joint sixth place (with Colin Goody) in the Championship of Sussex, which had a field of 16 starters. The Sussex title is one of the oldest in British speedway, first contested in 1932 and over the decades raced at whatever level the track was competing at, being won by such notable riders as Wally Green, Merv Hannam, Ray Cresp, Neil Middleditch, Martin Dugard, Andrew Silver and Bjarne Pedersen.

His last recorded SAL appearances of 1957 came over the weekend of Saturday and Sunday 7/8 September. On the Saturday evening at Aldershot's Tongham Stadium, Rye House were again heavily beaten by 60 points to 23 and Mauger failed to score in three rides, suffering two engine failures. The following day, at Hoddesdon, his return was one point and one engine failure as Rye House beat the Shots 48-35.

The Mauger family spent the winter of 1957/58 together in the UK, with Ivan taking a job as a van driver's mate with the Royal Arsenal Co-operative Society in Tooting Bec, taking him to every corner of London delivering groceries to the Society's shops.

When the 1958 season began the first indications were that it was unlikely to be much more successful for Ivan than the previous campaign, either in the National League or the Southern Area League. Midway through the season, the Maugers came to the conclusion that it would be best for Raye to take daughter Julie back to Christchurch, with Ivan staying in England and concentrating all his efforts on making some headway in speedway. The couple had to borrow money from their parents to pay Raye's fare back to New Zealand.

Although the parting was hard for a devoted family, Ivan's persistence eventually bore fruit as his form on the tracks that made up the Southern Area circuit blossomed forth in the second half of the '58 campaign.

The highlights for Wimbledon, if such they can be called, were appearances at The Firs, Norwich, when the Stars beat the Dons 72-48 in the National Trophy. Ten-man teams brought Ivan, Ernie Baker and Bobby Croombs into the Wimbledon team but the other two novices outpaced Mauger.

An immaculately turned-out speedway rider. Ivan Mauger, at Wimbledon's 1957 press day. Care of his equipment and personal appearance was to be a hallmark of Mauger's career. (Peter Morrish (John Somerville Collection.)

Ivan scored two points when he was included in the return leg of the Trophy at Plough Lane. Wimbledon won the match 67-53 but lost 125-115 on aggregate. Further team appeances for the Dons came in a challenge match against Southampton and in a National League match against Oxford late in the season, when Mauger fell in his first ride and failed to score.

There was no actual Southern Area League in 1958, due to a lack of interested teams, but the surviving Sunday training tracks put together a programme of challenge matches and individual events to keep the riders occupied and the fans happy.

On 11 May Ivan was at Eastbourne, scoring five points in the Championship of Sussex, won by Frank Bettis, who had spells with West Ham, Middlesbrough and Rayleigh and much experience at SAL level. On 8 June Eastbourne entertained the little known training track side Chiswick Nomads, with Ivan scoring eight paid nine points against a visiting side including men who went on to have rewarding league careers , such as Leo McAuliffe, Tommy Sweetman and Clive Hitch.

Ivan now established himself in the Eastbourne Eagles team for the rest of the 1958 challenge match season and began to enjoy some real success at the level. He notched up

Opposite: *Words of encouragement from Wimbledon star Ron How. (Peter Morrish/ John Somerville Collection.)*

Mauger in press day action from Wimbledon in 1957. (John Somerville Collection.)

Ivan on the Southern Area League circuit, a picture probably taken at Arlington Stadium, Eastbourne. Despite struggling in the SAL in 1957, Ivan enjoyed considerable success in 1958 (when there was no actual Southern Area League but plenty of challenge and individual action at the tracks). In the background, just behind Ivan, is Tommy Sweetman. (John Chaplin/John Somerville Collection.)

11 points when the Eagles beat a Coventry second team, nine points against a Southampton select and a first full maximum in Eastbourne's 51-33 home victory over California.

Individually he did well too, scoring 11 points in the qualifying heats of the Silver Helmet at Arlington on 3 August. He qualified for the final and won it, defeating McAuliffe, Colin Goody and Jim Gleed. The first, albeit modest international recognition of his career came when he was selected for Young Overseas in their 58-49 defeat by a Young England side at Arlington on 31 August.

Success continued into September 1958, when he recorded a paid maximum in a challenge match against Rye House and at Eastbourne's final meeting of the season he lifted the Supporters' Trophy, with a paid maximum.

Although the financial pickings from this run of success would have been relatively small, with the SAL paying around ten shillings a point, the boost to Ivan's morale of such unprecedented track success must have been enormous. Although no doubt the desire to be reunited with his family was a strong inducement to go back to New Zealand for the winter, why was there no question of a return to England in 1959?

New Zealand speedway writer Tracy Holmes says Mauger made the reasons for his non-return crystal clear in later years. In his book *Triple Crown Plus* (Pelham Books ISBN 9780720705284) Ivan explained that he made it clear that if anyone wanted him back in England for the 1959 season they would have to find the money to bring his wife over as well. Mauger said:

It wasn't that I believed I was that good, it was just that I would rather forget about English speedway than to be separated from my wife and family.

Tracy Holmes believes the lack of any interest from either Ronnie Greene or any other British promoter proved in the long run to be in Ivan's own interests, saying:

Ivan's refusal to return to England unless whoever wanted to sign him paid for his family as well turned out to be the best thing that could have happened. It led to the time when Ivan, his brother Trevor, his best friend Bernie Lagrosse and another mate, Ivan Crozier, all went to Australia.

Ivan's friendship with Jack Young in this Australian apprenticeship did him more good than any league experience in Britain could have done. In those years, Young taught him everything there was to know and Ivan absorbed the lot! So when Mike Parker signed him for Provincial League Newcastle for the 1963 season, he was more than ready for the task ahead .

(Ivan Mauger's contribution to the Provincial League will be described in detail in Chapter Ten, *1963 Disputes, Farewell and Mauger's Return.*)

Chapter 5
SOWING THE SEEDS OF REVIVAL

ALTHOUGH the establishment of the Provincial League in 1960 was the acknowledged turning point for the fortunes of speedway in Great Britain, arguably rescuing the sport, if not from imminent collapse but perhaps rather from stagnation, the seeds of the revival had been sown intermittently throughout the 1950s.

Outside the ranks of the National League and the Southern Area League, these seeds began to bear some substantial fruit in 1959, the last year of what had proved to be a tumultuous decade for the sport.

The period embracing the middle and latter years of the 1950s is usually represented as a dark time for speedway and it would be wrong to downplay the difficulties the sport encountered. But outside the National League and the Southern Area League there was a surprising amount of speedway activity.

The enormous amount of research carried out by speedway historians and published through the excellent medium of the *Speedway Researcher* magazine and website has revealed just how much racing outside the league structures did take place throughout the decade, some of which was examined in detail in Chapters One and Two, *True Grit Kept Speedway Alive in the North* and *Feast and Famine for Tartan Trackmen*.

Speedway outside the leagues, on an open licence (and occasionally *without* official approval), was in fact staged at no fewer than 30 centres during the 1950s, with the venues ranging from the vast open bowl of Bradford's Odsal Stadium and the impressive metropolitan stadia of Harringay and New Cross down to the rustic arenas of California in England, near Wokingham in Berkshire and Ringwood in the New Forest.

There were always enthusiasts, many of them former riders, willing to invest their time and cash in staging speedway. In some cases tracks which found it impossible to continue with the costs of league racing chose the immediate option of an open licence, with challenge matches and individual events providing continuity for the fans. In other cases revivals were staged, with varying success, after the tracks had lain fallow for several years.

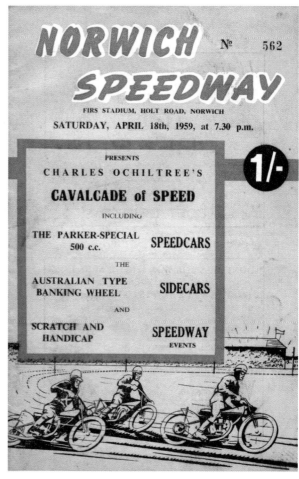

Cavalcade of Speed events were promoted not only on unlicensed tracks in 1959 but were also organised by leading promoters and administrators such as Charles Ochiltree and staged at National League circuits. This is the programme for an event at The Firs, Norwich. (Mike Kemp.)

An early example of a brief season of 'pirate' meetings involved Long Eaton, the track where, despite being situated in a heavily populated area midway between the large centres of Derby and Nottingham, had withdrawn from the Southern League (the former National League Division Three) mid-season in 1952. Attendances at the Station Road track had dipped just below the 4000 mark, a mouth-watering figure in the year 2020 but insufficient in the days of punitive entertainment tax.

In 1953 former Norwich rider Paddy Mills (real name Horace Burke) ran speedway practice sessions at Brafield but when Brafield joined the Southern Area League in 1954 he transferred his training activities to Long Eaton. Refused a licence for competitive racing at Station Road, he nevertheless staged three 'pirate' meetings using an assortment of riders, some racing openly and others using assumed names. Johnny Jones, a Long Eaton team man in the early 1950s, lost his licence as a result of being honest about his identity, whilst the others seem to have escaped punishment.

Mike Parker spent the 1959 speedway season at odds with the National League promoters, who objected to the unlicensed meetings he promoted at Liverpool, Bradford Odsal and Cradley Heath. That did not however stop those same promoters from hiring his speedcars for use in composite Cavalcade of Speed meetings on licensed tracks. Parker was one of speedway's 'flying squad' and is pictured in the cockpit of his private aeroplane. (J Spencer Oliver/John Somerville Collection.)

In the middle years of the decade there were the previously-mentioned short-lived open licence revivals at Middlesbrough (1953-58), Glasgow (1956), Exeter (1957-58), Liverpool (1957), Yarmouth 1957-58 and Motherwell (1958). It must also not be forgotten that the traditional Sunday afternoon tracks at Eastbourne (which had presented speedway at some level every year with the exception of the World War Two period since 1928) and Rye House, established in 1934, ran on an open licence basis in the seasons of the 1950s when the Southern Area League was not functioning.

The track revivals expanded both in numbers and geographical location in 1959, with speedway staged that year at a total of 24 venues, giving the sport its highest number of operating tracks for many years. In addition to the nine venues in the National League – Wimbledon, Leicester, Coventry, Norwich, Southampton, Poole, Oxford, Swindon and Belle Vue (in finishing order), the SAL had its healthiest number of contestants since the league was formed in 1954, with Eastbourne, Yarmouth, Aldershot, Rye House and Ipswich completing their fixtures.

Racing at open licence venues in 1959 varied enormously in terms of the grade of racing and the numbers of meetings staged. Heading the list where some of the old glamour and showmanship of the glory years could be experienced was the South London venue of New Cross, once one of the London 'big five' Division One teams. Johnnie Hoskins, still at the time manager at Belle Vue, opened the venue on 19 August and ran eight meetings.

The challenge matches and individual events mostly featured National League riders but there opportunities too at New Cross for juniors. The programmes at the track also included reserve matches and other second half events and these attracted a host of riders from both the SAL clubs and further afield.

Hoskins opened the season with a challenge match, New Cross Rangers v Wimbledon Dons, reviving a London derby fixture last seen in 1953. Wimbledon fielded a full National League side, including former World champion Ronnie Moore, whilst Hoskins

On a large track and in the right conditions sidecars could be as spectacular as speedcars. The machines, using Australian-style hinged chairs for the passenger to aid cornering, are pictured during a second half event at Belle Vue. (Mike Kemp.)

New Zealander and former Wembley rider Trevor Redmond, pictured on his houseboat on the River Thames, was another promoter in the spotlight during the revival year of 1959. An enthusiastic stager of the sport outside the National League system, he ran meetings at Bristol and St Austell that year, as well as riding for Swindon. (Alf Weedon/ John Somerville Collection.)

had trawled the National League for the men to represent the Rangers. Another former World Champion in Peter Craven was in his side, along with a future title holder in Bjorn Knutsson. New Cross won the match 47-43.

In many ways the line-ups for the reserve team matches were more interesting (and certainly less predictable) than those for the main events. Southern juniors got a chance to race in an impressive stadium, with New Cross Reserves including Reg Luckhurst and Bobby Croombs whilst Ernie Baker and John Leggett represented the Dons. The most intriguing members of the New Cross reserve side were northerners Malcolm Bruce and Tommy Roper, most probably known to Hoskins from Belle Vue.

During the second halves of the remaining New Cross meetings of 1959 a score of names of other men who would find team places in Provincial League teams seeds featured, both in reserve matches and other second half events. Some were based in London and the south of England, with Vic White, Clive Hitch, Stan Stevens, Eric Hockaday among them but a rare visitor was Ray Wickett, later associated with St Austell and Plymouth.

Throughout the late 1950s Redmond and his father-in-law Bob Netcott promoted open licence speedway at the homely Cornish Stadium in St Austell, during the peak holiday season. Trevor had ridden for Netcott at Aldershot at the start of his career. (John Somerville Collection.)

The track also staged the Speedway Riders Association (SRA) Trophy in the second half of a challenge match against an All Stars team. This was contested by, among others, Ivor Brown, Ross Gilbertson, Stan Stevens,Tommy Sweetman, Gil Goldfinch and Pete Jarman. The final and the trophy went to Ivor Brown, ahead of Stevens, Gilbertson and Jarman.

Exceeding New Cross in terms of the number of meetings staged was the south western outpost of St Austell. The Gulls, based at the homely Cornish Stadium, had opened on an open licence in 1949 and enjoyed four seasons of league racing in first National League Division Three and the successor Southern League in the period 1950-53 inclusive.

After dropping out of the sport for five years, a Cornish revival was led by Trevor Redmond and his father-in-law Bob Netcott, who had been promoter at Aldershot, where the Kiwi star began his career. The duo ran St Austell on an open licence from 1958 to 1961, operating mainly during the peak holiday months of July and August, when Cornwall was full of holidaymakers, including many from speedway areas.

In 1959 St Austell ran no fewer than eleven meetings, more than double those actually staged in the rain-hit summer of the previous year. Like at New Cross, the main events mainly featured riders from the National League, with all the biggest names – Craven, Fundin, Ronnie Moore and many others happy to make the long journey to the South West long before the motorway system was developed.

Bristol, out of the sport since withdrawing from National League Division Two at the end of 1955, was revived by promoters Jack Nott, Eric Salmon and Bill Hamblin. The first meeting, on 15 May 1959 was an individual event, the Bristol Challenge Bowl, won by Ronnie Moore with a 15 point maximum.

Knowle Stadium staged eight meetings up to the end of August. Unlike other revived tracks, where the presence of the National League star men designed to draw the crowds was supplemented by a reasonable diet of racing for second strings and juniors, Bristol concentrated for the most part on the big names. A major draw for the West Country fans was the inclusion of former Bulldogs Dick Bradley, comeback man Johnny Hole, and Cliff Cox.

Bristol took part in one team event away from Knowle, finishing last in a three-team tournament at St Austell which also involved the home side and a team representing Exeter, including the Falcons' former Australian stars Jack Geran and Neil Street and local man Francis Cann. This meeting featured a race for St Austell juniors Chris Julian, Lewis Philp and Ivor Toms.

Plymouth was ranked next in terms of number of meetings staged, with five, including four challenge matches and a Best Pairs contest at Pennycross Stadium, promoted by the Trevor Redmond/Bob Netcott combination. The first meeting, on 27 March saw the Plymouth Devils lose narrowly to a team labelled as The Midlands, although with the noted exception of Leicester's Harry Bastable most of the riders were southern-based. The Plymouth side included former Pennycross favourites Pete Lansdale and Alan Smith and also former Harringay and Wembley personality Split Waterman.

Four World Champions, Ronnie Moore, Peter Craven, Barry Briggs and Ove Fundin, raced at Pennycross in 1959, together with many other leading National League men, giving the West Country crowd a treat rarely enjoyed since the mid-1930s, when Plymouth were members of the one division National League of the time.

There were, nevertheless, plenty of opportunities for juniors at Plymouth. The British Best Pairs meeting at the end of April included a junior event featuring Francis Cann and Ron Tuck, Chris Julian and Jack Board, and Charlie Wallis and Peter Burgess. Most meetings included second half junior events.

It is interesting to note that although 1959 is usually remembered as the season of the Mike Parker-promoted 'pirate' meetings at tracks in the north and the Midlands, three of the four open licence venues mentioned so far in this chapter were in the West Country and one in London. Add to the aforementioned list single meetings at Harringay, and Rayleigh and it will be seen that, out of 43 open licence meetings staged in Britain in 1959 no fewer than 34 were in the South and South West.

The hard fact is that, although it is the Mike Parker 'pirate' meetings that have passed into speedway legend, in reality they numbered only eight events at three venues – four at Odsal, Bradford, three at Liverpool and one at Cradley Heath. The one other 1959 meeting yet to be mentioned took place at Old Meadowbank, Edinburgh, organised to raise funds for the local university students' charity appeal.

Numbers, however, are not the whole story. With few of the northern riders of the 1950s ever venturing to the South of England, either to seek team places in SAL sides or to compete for second half bookings, the meetings at Odsal, Stanley Stadium and Dudley Wood sent an important signal to the Northern men, perhaps hit hardest of all by speedway's slump, that someone was prepared to do something about their plight.

Subsequent chapters will show that although neither Bradford nor Liverpool tore up many trees in the new competition, their re-opening aroused interest in other long defunct northern centres – notably Sheffield and Newcastle, where the Tigers and the Diamonds respectively eventually took their places in the PL and still survive and thrive in the sport today. The other track to benefit from Mike Parker's attention in 1959, Cradley Heath, would no doubt still be thriving in British speedway had not the stadium succumbed to the developers.

Parker, at least initially, had little or no interest in speedway. After experience of deep sea fishing on trawlers based at Fleetwood, close to his Blackpool birthplace, he served in the Merchant Navy in World War Two and on demobilisation turned initially to the building trade, eventually building up a variety of business interests including shops, a property company, a building and contracting concern and a self-drive hire company.

His connection with short circuit racing came as a result of a meeting in Manchester with Johnnie Hoskins, who encouraged him to drive a stock car. After destroying several cars in the rough and tumble that was stock car racing in its early days in the UK, Parker turned to midget cars, or speedcars as they were often known in Britain.

Journalist Cyril J Hart described how Parker came to consider the possibility of becoming a speedway promoter. Hart, who as secretary of the Speedway Riders Association in the late 1950s played a considerable role in the creation of the Provincial League, said:

Trevor Redmond is pictured returning to the pits at St Austell, where the holidaying spectators stood on grass banks under the trees, in an atmosphere similar to that at Southern Area League venues. (Sally Chandler.)

As a midget car driver Parker began to mix freely with speedway riders and the sport's public and at a supporters' dance in Manchester he had a long and earnest discussion with Peter Craven. It was Peter, possibly with thoughts that midgets didn't mix as well as they should with pure speedway, who first suggested to Parker that he should find his own track or tracks for the presentation of midgets. That is how Mike first came to open the Odsal circuit at Bradford, in association with Jess Halliday.

Parker was never a speedway man, pure and simply. When Bradford re-opened in 1959 it was his intention to present the four-wheelers. But he soon discovered that the nucleus of his patrons wanted speedway as well, and some even went so far as to say that they preferred speedway to the cars.

On the basis of giving the paying customers what they wanted to see, Parker approached the Speedway Control Board for the necessary permits and licenses, but was turned down. The rebuff was essentially the catalyst for the Provincial League.

Bradford was the first venue to be opened by Parker and Jess Halliday. Saturday 6 June 1959 was the date for the first meeting at Odsal since the end of September 1957. It was a Cavalcade of Speed event (no-one seems to have claimed copyright over the title, which was used quite widely in the era), consisting partly of speedway races featuring Parker and Halliday's band of northern juniors. Vic Lonsdale, Ted Connor, Roy Peacock, Arthur Rowe, Sonny Dewhirst and others took part in a Roses Match, Yorkshire against Lancashire, with the White Rose county triumphing over the Red Roses of Lancashire by 33 points to 15. The bill of fare also included sidecar racing and Parker's speedcars, with Mike himself competing.

By the second meeting, on 4 July, some of the Yorkshire riders who were later to form the core of Bradford's 1960 Provincial League side – Stan Holey, Tommy Roper and Ray Day – were among the field competing for the Yorkshire Speedway Delegation Cup. Roper won the meeting with a 9pt maximum from his three rides.

Following a challenge match between Bradford and Liverpool later in July, with Yorkshire again coming out on top with a 41-30 victory, inspired by Stan Holey's 12 point maximum, the fourth and final meeting of the brief season introduced what appear to have been another set of speedway pirates. On Saturday 22 August, with the Stars racing National League and Reserve League fixtures at The Firs against Poole, a team using the name Norwich were the visitors to Odsal in a challenge match, with Bradford winning 41-28.

Leading scorers for Norwich were veteran Geoff Pymar and the promising Ron Bagley, who in 1959 rode for Ipswich in the Southern Area League. The fact that Pymar and Bagley, together with other less well known team mates were licensed riders appearing on a 'pirate' track in an unlicensed meeting for a supposedly renegade promoter in the form of Parker, raises the question of whether their actions put *their* racing permits at risk?

Mike Parker opened Liverpool on 29 July with, inevitably, a challenge match against stable mates Bradford, who won the encounter by 42 points to 29. The teams on parade that night were similar to the men who would represent the two sides at the start of the Provincial League – Dave Gerrard, Bert Edwards, Roy Peacock, Ted Connor, Sonny Dewhurst and Arthur Rowe for Liverpool and Ray Day, Alan Forrest, Tommy Roper, Tony Barnard, Vic Lonsdale, Stan Holey and Ricky Smith for Bradford.

Following the Merseyside Championship individual meeting at Stanley Stadium on 25 August, won by Derek Skyner, with Ray Day as runner-up, Liverpool saw its third and last 1959 meeting on 23 September. The visiting team was again racing under the title of Norwich, but unlike at Bradford earlier in the season the nickname Rebels (very apt in the circumstances) was added.

The only recognisable name in the Norwich line-up was that of Odsal rider Vic Lonsdale, loaned to the visitors for the evening. Speedway's records seem to have little mention of the rest of the Rebels team – Rupert Roc, Toy (perhaps Tony?) Woolwich, Barry Williams, Van Murad and a reserve shown simply as Davis, who won his only ride. Pymar and Bagley were absent on this occasion. For the record, the Norwich Rebels won 39-31.

The final meeting of the 'pirate' series was at Cradley Heath on 29 August, promoted by Parker and Halliday in association with stadium lessees Fred and Morris Jephcott. A side racing under the name of Cradley Heath Midlanders drew 35-35 with Bradford. Despite the 'Midlanders' title, the participants were all part of the Parker group of Northern juniors. Assistance with the organisation of the meeting was apparently given to the Jephcotts by a well-known legitimate rider/promoter, who saw fit to withdraw at an appropriate time before the tapes went up to avoid being associated with an unlicensed meeting.

Looking back over the years some significant questions are raised by Parker's activities during the 1959 speedway season. Although he cocked a snook at speedway officialdom by running unlicensed meetings, there is considerable evidence that at the same time he maintained a business relationship with the National League promoters with whom he was theoretically at odds.

Parker's contacts with National League tracks extended across most of the 1959 season and were mostly concerned with speedcars. A feature of 1959 was the number of Cavalcade of Speed composite meetings held across the country. In April, before the Parker 'pirate' meetings got underway, Norwich's Firs Stadium staged a meeting under the title 'Charles Ochiltree's Cavalcade of Speed', suggesting that the Coventry chief had some interest in the promotion of the event. This featured some heats of solo speedway, sidecars and the speedcars controlled by Mike Parker.

As the season progressed Charles Ochiltree staged three composite meetings at Brandon, in March under the branding of 'Disciples of Dice' (the type of title the CO routinely gave to his extremely successful stock car meetings), on 15 August and again on 26 September. Other National League tracks to stage Cavalcade of Speed-type meetings using Parker's speedcars (and, as had been the case at Coventry, including Parker himself among the competitors) included Oxford and Swindon.

The National League promoters seemed prepared to do business with Parker despite his defiance of the speedway authorities. At Belle Vue the cars had been part of Hyde Road second halves since 1956. No doubt the Cavalcade of Speed meetings at the National League tracks brought welcome additional income into the coffers and there is probably another reason why the league's promoters were prepared to co-operate with Parker and hire his cars whilst at the same time giving him the cold shoulder when it came to speedway.

The speedway media generally took the side of the National League promoters when Mike Parker defied the Control Board's refusal of a licence for Bradford and Liverpool and, with a group of Northern juniors decided to 'run black'. (Ted Connor Collection.)

A POINT OF VIEW FROM JOHN HYAM

"A sport with a strong Control Board maintains its respect and is recognised by other organisations. Speedway is fortunate to have a wise ruling body, one that works without fear or favour in the interests of speedway racing."

A word of praise

I like the Board's tough policy

SPEEDWAY gets more exciting everyday. Bradford although refused a licence by the Speedway Control Board

The controlling authority of   Ah! The side-car drivers.

The Star *editor's opinion piece soon produced a reply from Ted Connor, acting as a spokesman for the Northern junior riders who linked up with Parker. (Ted Connor Collection.)*

SPEEDWAY STAR & NEWS, July 25, 1959

DO NOT CONDEMN US!
pleads TED CONNOR (Liverpool)

JOHN HYAM'S recent article criticising Bradford, and its unlicenced riders must be answered, and as one of the riders involved, I feel that I am just the man for the job.

It was probably argued that the 'pirate' speedway meetings were in direct defiance of the Control Board. But where the speedcars were concerned there was no governing body to flout!

Speedway Star had nailed its colours to the mast as early as June 1959. In a comment piece headed *'I like the Board's tough policy'*, editor John Hyam had a taken a dim view of Parker and Halliday's defiance of the Speedway Control Board. He said:

Bradford, although refused a licence [by the SCB] ran a mixed meeting on 6 June, featuring solos and midget cars. The solo riders who rode in this meeting have been banned from appearance on any tracks licensed by the Board. Which is a fair action, for the Board must maintain its government of the sport in this country on behalf of the Auto Cycle Union and the FIM (The Fédération Internationale de Motocyclisme).

'Flapping tracks' are a source of annoyance to greyhound racing and chances are that similar circuits operating outside the recognised speedway authorities would be a thorn in the side of organised speedway. Suspension of the solo riders who participated at Bradford was the only action the Control Board could take. Yet the midget car drivers get away without any disciplinary action being taken against them, as there is no controlling authority for that sport in this country.

The speedway press nevertheless accepted advertising when Parker launched his 'pirate' meetings. (Ted Connor Collection.)

STANLEY STADIUM
PRESCOT ROAD   LIVERPOOL

MIKE PARKER presents
THE OPENING MEETING OF THE SEASON
with

LIVERPOOL v. **BRADFORD**
PIRATES   PANTHERS

CHALLENGE MATCH

—PLUS—

Guest Riders including
DENT OLIVER
and
THE SENSATIONAL

SPEEDCARS

Britain's New Fast and Furious Sport
Featuring British Champion
BRUCE BLOOD
EIGHT CAR FINAL

TEAM RACES

Wednesday, 29th JULY, 7.30 p.m.
Admission: 2/-, 3/-, 4/-. Grandstand 5/-. Children's Paddock 1/-.

The *Star's* approval for the action taken against the Parker/Halliday juniors who had raced in the pirate meetings was answered by a letter from one of the banned riders, Ted Connor (Liverpool) who was to go on to play a leading role in the negotiations which eventually led to unlicensed Northern juniors being accepted into the Speedway Riders Association (SRA). Ted pleaded:

Do not condemn us! The riders fully appreciate that they have done wrong by racing on an unlicensed circuit. But it must also be remembered that the many juniors in the North of England have no Southern Area League to compete in. There is no intention by the riders competing at Bradford or

Liverpool of bringing any disrepute on the sport. We all love speedway far too much for that to be allowed to happen.

Before we raced at Bradford (which is not a 'flapping track') we were concerned about the conditions we should race under. These Mike Parker has met to the very letter. Pay rates are better than in the Southern Area League. Bradford's dressing room facilities and track organisation are beyond reproach, our insurance rates are the same as on the National League tracks (Parker paid the premiums in full) and the supper laid on for the riders after the first meeting at Odsal was fit for a king.

While we are only juniors and cannot dictate our own terms, we do see that we ride under conditions which will not disgrace our sport.

The speedway press in the summer of 1959, although the plans for the Provincial League were in a very early stage and the title does not appear to have been mentioned as such, nevertheless contained several suggestions that the sport was on the verge of an exciting expansion. On 27 June - two months before the 'pirate' meeting at Dudley Wood - the *Star* reported that Cradley Heath had applied for a licence with the intention of entering the National League in 1960. The magazine commented:

Things look good for the sport. There is no reason why next year should not feature a twelve team National League embracing this year's [nine] participants plus Ipswich, Bristol and Cradley Heath.

Don't be surprised if applications are also made by Liverpool and Middlesbrough with a view to staging National League racing in 1960. One thing is certain; if these tracks re-open there will have to be a complete re-pooling of riding talent, and teams will probably have to sign at least two Continentals apiece to help balance team strengths.

Just a month later and the *Star's* fairly confident predictions of a major expansion for the National League had been toned down, with the magazine commenting:

Chances are that 1960 will see a Northern League embracing Liverpool, Bradford, Sheffield, Stoke, Middlesbrough and possibly Edinburgh in operation.

The new prediction was a more accurate guess at the constitution of any new competition. But the Control Board's prompt action in banning the riders on the Parker / Halliday circuit indicated that there was a long way to go before speedway was able to reverse its period of closures and grow once again.

Liverpool's Stanley Stadium staged the speedway challenge match with its added attractions, as advertised in the Speedway Star, *on 29 July 1959. (Author's Collection.)*

The Liverpool squad for the 1959 challenge matches v Bradford at Stanley Stadium. Pictured standing, l-r, are Dave Gerrard, Roy Maddock, Arthur Rowe, Norman Murray, Bert Edwards. Kneeling, l-r, Roy Peacock, Sonny Dewhirst, Derek Skyner, Ted Connor. (Ted Connor Collection.)

Whilst looking in detail at the sport in 1959 it would be wrong to ignore the one really positive area of expansion approved by the powers-that-be. The National League Reserve League was a well-meaning development and provided plenty of additional rides for juniors, although it did end in relative failure.

All nine of the National League's clubs took part in the Reserve League, although at one stage that did not appear likely and, speedway being speedway, there was a dispute which could have led to a farcical position.

Speedway Star reported the bombshell news that Belle Vue manager Johnnie Hoskins, for an undisclosed reason, had opposed the new competition and the response of the authorities was to serve him with a notice that unless he *did* stage reserve matches, the Hyde Road club would have its racing licence cancelled!

The management at Belle Vue, with its traditionally busy second halves, where the introduction of such attractions as Parker's speedcars, sidecars and scramble bikes appeared to have done little to stop the flow of promising young riders coming off the Hyde Road production line, did not always take kindly to being dictated to.

According to the *Star*, the notice caused little more than 'mild amusement' in Manchester and the article said the intriguing point about the Board's notice seemed to be whether, if Hoskins had held out over the Reserve League, would the authorities *really* have closed the track? The magazine's reporter asked:

Would one of the few money-spinners in the sport be closed on this sort of issue?

The format decided upon was for the reserve teams to each have four riders, with the matches, raced over five heats, taking place after the interval on dates when the first teams involved has been in action earlier in the programme. The scheme actually provided competitive racing for more than 90 riders, both National League second strings and juniors, plus familiar names drafted in from

Tapes up during an unlicensed meeting at Liverpool in 1959. (Ted Connor Collection.)

Crowds on the Odsal, Bradford, terraces as Ted Connor competes in a 1959 'pirate' meeting. (Ted Connor Collection.)

Ted Connor (seen left) vouched for this picture as being taken during the unlicensed meeting at Cradley Heath on 29 August 1959. The event featured a match between Midlanders and Bradford (a 35-35 draw), although Connor and his team-mate are wearing Liverpool racejackets. All the riders were drawn from Mike Parker's Liverpool and Bradford squads. (Ted Connor Collection.)

the Southern Area League. Norwich used a total of 15 riders whilst Poole managed with just seven.

The status and level of experience of the riders varied enormously. Phil Clarke, World Finalist, England international and scorer of more than 2000 points for Norwich during his twelve-year career at The Firs, made several appearances in Stars' reserve side in what was to prove his final season.

Other top flight riders to appear over the season included another former World Finalist and Test star for Australia, Graham Warren, and Nigel Boocock (for Coventry), Howdy Byford and Ken Adams, former National League Division One riders for West Ham and Wembley respectively, and many more. Some riders appeared for more than one reserve side with Ivor Brown, at the time appearing in the SAL for Yarmouth, turning out for Leicester (eight appearances), Norwich and Wimbledon.

Sadly, the National Reserve League fixtures, which envisaged 16 matches, each team racing eight home and eight away matches, were not completed. Leicester, after racing eleven matches, finished top of the table, for what it was worth. Swindon, who managed to ride the most fixtures (13) were bottom.

Despite the arguments, the banning of Northern juniors simply desperate for a chance of some competitive racing on proper tracks, the only relative success of the Reserve League and the many wide of the mark predictions about the future of the sport, speedway in 1959 had moved from a rather stolid acceptance of its reduced status to a renewed belief that better times *just might* be around the corner.

When the last match of 1959 was raced, the action moved from the track and pits into smoke-filled committee rooms. Could the rifts in the sport be healed, and could a new league herald happier days ahead?

Chapter 6

WINNERS AND LOSERS AS COMPETITION TAKES SHAPE

THE late John Wick, the experienced editor for many years of *Speedway World* and secretary of the Southern Area League Promoters' Association, left behind a vivid first-person description of the moves in the winter months of 1959-1960 which led to the birth of the Provincial League.

The meetings at Bradford, Liverpool and Cradley had not only aroused interest among the fans at those venues who had turned out in substantial numbers. Across the country other venues and other would-be promoters, particularly those running the Southern Area League tracks, had taken careful note of the success of Parker and his associates.

The SAL had filled a vital role in the South of England but had for the most part struggled to maintain a viable membership. Adding Bradford, Liverpool and Cradley to the 1959 Southern Area League tracks, with the strong possibility that other northern

Key figure number one at the Speedway Control Board. Lt Colonel R Vernon C Brook, chairman of the Board during the negotiations that led to approval for the Provincial League to operate in 1960. Colonel Brook, fourth from left, was a familiar figure at British tracks in the 1950s and is pictured presenting the Midland Riders Championship trophy to Graham Warren of Birmingham (left). Others in the picture, l-r are Jack Parker, Birmingham promoter Les Marshall, and Charles Ochiltree of Coventry. (Alf Weedon/John Somerville Collection.)

Key figure number two at the Speedway Control Board. Major W W 'Bill' Fearnley (second from left) presents the Golden Helmet to Split Waterman of Harringay, during a Racers v Bristol National League match. (Harringay Unattributed/John Somerville Collection.)

venues would emerge for 1960, offered the SAL chiefs the tempting prospect of truly competitive competition and an expanded fixture list. John Wick recalled:

> The first thing was to arrange a meeting between Parker and Halliday and the SAL promoters, to persuade them to drop their policy of running meetings without the authority of the Control Board and get them to agree to abide by the official regulations. This was not going to be an easy task, for Mike [Parker] had openly declared that he had no time for the Control Board or their methods.

Parker and Halliday nevertheless agreed to a meeting and when it took place the northerners were introduced to Wick and promoters Charlie Dugard of Eastbourne, Fred Peachey of Rye House, Alf Weedon (Yarmouth) and John Pilblad (Aldershot). The gathering was also attended by Trevor Redmond, who had kept St Austell alive with open licence meetings and had gained huge experience of promoting speedway in a setting far from big populations and with difficulties of access in pre-motorway (and even dual carriageway) days.

John Wick went on to describe how Parker, clearly encouraged by the enthusiasm of the SAL men, and with the knowledge of other tracks, including Stoke, ready to re-open, said he was prepared to throw his tracks into a new league, providing the Control Board would be co-operative. Wick added:

> So far, things had gone better than expected, mainly due to Parker being prepared to listen to the other side of the argument. I spoke to Major Bill Fearnley, Control Board secretary and then wrote to Lt Colonel Vernon Brook, the Board's

chairman, requesting an exploratory meeting with the suggested Provincial League promoters. To our delight he replied that he would be pleased to meet us, on the understanding that he could give no assurances without first consulting the Board's other members.

The meeting took place soon after Christmas, at the Control Board's offices in Brewer Street, London. Both sides were prepared to make concessions and the outcome was that the Control Board announced that it was prepared to sanction the formation of the Provincial League.

When the outbreak of peace became widely known applications came from would-be promoters from across the country. The inaugural meetings of the new league were now held in Manchester, either in the flat above Parker's hardware shop in the Moss Side district or at the Palm Court Restaurant and pub at the main gate of the Belle Vue entertainment complex.

Attending the meetings were the men willing to sign up for the Provincial League – some currently established as promoters and others who had considerable past experience. Wally Mawdsley and Pete Lansdale applied for Rayleigh and Charles Foot and Jack Knott expressed interest for Poole and Bristol. Ian Hoskins heard of the proposal for a new league through father Johnnie, at the heart of things at Belle Vue and wasted no time in leasing Edinburgh's Old Meadowbank Stadium. Frank Varey was interested

More key figures in the intensive talks that led up to the birth of the Provincial League. Johnnie Hoskins (left) would be involved in son Ian's promotion at Edinburgh from 1960, Mike Parker (centre) had been at the heart of planning for the new league whilst Bradford rider Norman Redmond (right) played an important role in the negotiations between the riders who had raced in Parker's 'pirate' meetings and the Speedway Riders Association (SRA) which urged them to become legitimate. (Author's Collection.)

How the Speedway press reported the meeting in Manchester where the formerly unlicensed Northern riders agreed to join the Speedway Riders' Association. (Ted Connor Collection.)

Momentous meeting held in Manchester
Northern Riders join the S.R.A.

After terms had been agreed between the unlicensed riders and the Riders Association Ted Connor (right) was appointed as the SRA's representative in the North of England. He is pictured in 1960 in the Stoke pits with Potters' team-mate, Bill Bridgett, later a key associate of Mike Parker. (Author's Collection.)

in promoting at Sheffield and the Jephcotts of Cradley Heath, associated with Parker in 1959, also lodged an application.

Former West Ham and Stoke rider Reg Fearman, now back in the UK after his time in New Zealand, had become involved in October 1959. Fearman, who was to hold the highest offices in British speedway during his long career as promoter and administrator, explains:

> Dave Anderson, who had ridden for Hanley (Stoke) in the late 1940s and still lived in the area, called into my garage business in the Potteries to ask if I was interested in riding again. He told me that Mike Parker was planning to revive speedway at Sun Street in Hanley, which was the scene of some of my best racing memories.
>
> I met Parker during the winter of 1959-60 and we did a deal to promote Stoke on a fifty/fifty basis through a company we formed named Northern Speedways Limited. I set about installing all the equipment needed to stage speedway racing, including the track lighting system.

With interest being declared by thirteen tracks and the Control Board giving its approval, the new league offered the prospect of speedway in Britain more than doubling its size in one fell swoop. But there were many more obstacles to overturn before the racing could begin, not the least being the attitude of the Northern riders who had performed for Parker, Halliday and their other associates outside the rule of authority. John Wick remembered:

> The former 'pirate' track riders had done well out of their 1959 season, without any strings being attached. Would they, as their promoters had agreed to do, accept

Race you to the line! Bill Bridgett (left) and Mike Parker forsake speedway bikes and speedcars respectively for track grading equipment. (Alf Weedon/John Somerville Collection.)

There is a long tradition in British speedway of men who started out reporting the sport but became involved in promotion and administration. At the start of the Provincial League Cyril J Hart (pictured right) was editor of Speedway World *and secretary of the Speedway Riders' Association. He is seen presenting a trophy to Ivor Brown, one of the PL's earliest stars, watched over by Mike Parker. (John Somerville Collection.)*

Other journalists active in the sport in the 1950s and 1960s included the pipe-smoking Peter Arnold, also a leading announcer and the founder of what is now the World Speedway Riders Association, and Howard Jacobi, who covered the Midland tracks for the speedway media. (Alf Weedon/ John Somerville Collection.)

One of the best known photographers of the era was Alf Weedon, captured here by a fellow snapper. Weedon was also involved in promoting speedway, at Yarmouth. (John Somerville Collection.)

Welcome back to speedway! The start of the Provincial League brought riders, promoters and supporters back to the sport. Ian Hoskins (left) worked in industry after the Scottish tracks closed in the mid-1950s. Reg Fearman moved to New Zealand for a time.

Provincial League winners. A PL promoters' meeting showing the men who were granted licenses to operate at various stages of the competition's history. Pictured, back row, l-r, Ernest Palmer & Frank Varey (Sheffield), Pete Lansdale (Rayleigh/Exeter), Bernard Curtiss (Plymouth), Wally Mawdsley (Rayleigh/Exeter), Reg Fearman, Ian Hoskins, Morris Jephcott (Cradley), Dave Stevens, Johnnie Hoskins, Bill Bridgett (Wolverhampton), Jim Knott (Poole). Front row, Trevor Redmond, John Wick, Mike Parker, Charles Foot, Jack Knott. (Alf Weedon/John Somerville Collection.)

Eastbourne – like fellow PL rejects Rye House and Aldershot – continued to run open meetings. Charlie Dugard's sons Bob and John are pictured on the left in a Southern Area League era shot, believed to be from 1959. The full team is, l-r, Bob Dugard, John Dugard, Dave Still, Charlie Dugard, Bob Warner, Gil Goldfinch, Colin Gooddy, with Frank Bettis on the bike. (Peter Morrish/John Somerville Collection.)

the ruling of authority? Would they join the Speedway Riders' Association (SRA), obtain ACU competition licences and become bona fide speedway riders?

The agreement reached between the speedway authorities and Parker and his associates was soon matched by an understanding between the SRA and the northern juniors and novices. Two aspiring young Northern riders, Ted Connor and Norman Redmond, took the initiative and addressed meetings of their fellow riders, recognising the potential benefits of becoming legitimate.

The SRA – effectively the speedway riders' trade union – was at the time headed by the Wimbledon rider Cyril Brine. He took the decision to send the organisation's secretary, Cyril J Hart, to Manchester to negotiate with the men who had ridden for Parker in 1959. As with the negotiations between the Control Board and the potential PL promoters, concessions were made on both sides and agreement was reached.

Ted Connor was appointed as the SRA's northern representative, with a seat on the Association's executive committee, where he was later to be joined by Norman Redmond. Ted recalls:

Everything was legalised after the meeting with Cyril J Hart. The Provincial League was accepted, but initially at least with the exclusion of Ted Connor. I was to be made a scapegoat because of my leading role in 1959 in helping Mike Parker find sufficient riders for his unlicensed meetings and also because I had dared to ride in those meetings under my own name.

Thankfully for me, Parker put his foot down and said, no Ted Connor, no Provincial League under the Control Board. Because of that I was able to race at Stoke in the league's first season.

Connor's status as a scapegoat was soon removed, but there were to be some real losers amidst the euphoria which surrounded the start of the Provincial League and the long-term revival it brought about in British speedway, culminating in the British League and the new golden age for the sport of the 1970s

When congratulations all round appeared to be the order of the day, the Control Board dropped a bombshell. Ten tracks received the Board's blessing but three were refused licences. The Southern Area League teams that had applied to join the Provincial League – Rye House, Eastbourne and Aldershot – were rejected. In the case of Rye House and Eastbourne the Board ruled against them on the grounds that they raced on Sunday afternoons while the authorities claimed Aldershot's support for open licence speedway in 1959 would not meet the extra expense of running in a nationwide league.

Aldershot promoter John Pilblad (on tractor) who also lost out on the Provincial League worked tirelessly at the Hampshire circuit and at Weymouth over the years, with less success and reward than his passion for speedway deserved. (John Pilblad.)

*John Pilblad earned
more accolades in his
professional career than
from speedway. A top
outside-broadcast
cameraman, he is
pictured here with the
Prince of Wales. (John
Pilblad.)*

Dugard for Eastbourne and Peachey for Rye House appealed against the decision but the appeals failed. John Pilblad at Aldershot was however granted an open licence to allow him to prove there was a viable following at Tongham Stadium. Sadly, the disappointment felt by the Shots' fans at being excluded from the new league and the lack of really competitive racing led to poor crowds in 1960 and Aldershot was never to see speedway again, although it became a successful stock car racing venue.

Eastbourne and Rye House were 'given permission' by the Board to carry on with their Sunday challenge matches and individual events. It was to be many years before league racing became a reality at Hoddesdon and Arlington.

Today there is still sadness and amazement expressed at the exclusion of the three Southern Area League tracks from the PL. Did the leading role played by Dugard, Peachey and Pilblad in creating the new competition and expressing a willingness to link up with Parker count against them? Speaking today, Reg Fearman is scathing about the Board's decision, saying:

> With hindsight, it was criminal that the SAL tracks were refused. The Provincial League was not into its stride at that time otherwise as promoters we would not have accepted that decision of the SCB.

Not for the first (or the last) time in speedway, a triumph for the sport was marred by what appears to have been a mean and cruel action against the men from the Southern Area League who had played a major role throughout the turbulent 1950s in keeping the sport alive.

Chapter 7

1960: VETERANS V NOVICES CLASH AS PROVINCIAL LEAGUE IS BORN

ON Good Friday 15 April 1960, speedway history was made in two vividly contrasting locations.

The Provincial League raced its first fixtures, one in still largely rural Essex and the second more than 180 miles away in the heart of industrial England, amidst the closely-packed terraced houses and smoking bottle-shaped pot bank chimneys of Stoke-on-Trent.

Being speedway the new league was soon thrust into controversy, with the point at issue the age-old question of team strengths and whether the prime purpose of the new competition was to encourage new young talent or provide the chance of a comeback for men who had been forced out of the sport during the 1950s slump.

The gulf which existed at the start of the new competition between the tracks which resolved to adhere where possible to the policy of providing regular competitive rides for juniors and those which recruited men with considerable league experience, was highlighted from the very start.

The contest at Rayleigh Weir Stadium, opened in 1948 and situated some 6 miles from Southend-on-Sea, on the south side of the Southend Arterial Road, featured the local Rockets, a team which had managed to race fairly consistently during the 1950s, against Cradley Heath, where league speedway had last been seen in 1952.

Over at Sun Street in Hanley, the largest of the Five Towns of the Staffordshire Potteries made famous by the novels of Arnold Bennett (in reality there are six towns but Bennett used poetic licence) the second of the historic Provincial League opening fixtures was

The Weir Stadium, Rayleigh, Essex. (John Somerville Collection.)

Sun Street, Hanley, Stoke on Trent, packed to the rafters for the track's first meeting in the Provincial League. (John Somerville Collection.)

between Stoke Potters and Liverpool, both tracks controlled by the at that stage still amicable partnership of Mike Parker and Reg Fearman.

On that evening more than sixty years ago Bank Holiday speedway meetings were also taking place at three National League tracks, Leicester, Oxford and Wimbledon. But apart from the avid supporters gathered in those centres, the eyes of the speedway world in general were understandably focused firmly on the new Provincial League.

Speedway fans throughout the country wished the new venture well, although some of the most powerful people in the sport were yet to be convinced that the PL was a good idea. There was a school of thought, widely expressed over the previous months in the speedway media, that claimed the PL was a madcap venture, run by people without much experience of speedway administration, and probably doomed to failure.

It is time to leave the sport's internal politics behind and attempt to recreate some of the excitement surrounding the birth of the Provincial League. There were quite a few differences, quite apart from geographical location, between the two initial PL matches on that long-ago evening.

When Rayleigh paraded at The Weir the spectator with only a modest speedway knowledge could not avoid being aware that the team bearing the distinctive space rocket emblem was, on paper and, as it turned out on track, one of obvious strength. Rayleigh was one of the tracks which had refused to die during the height of the 1950s slump and in the decade the track had competed in all three Divisions of the National League and the Southern League. In 1957 The Weir had also staged fixtures for the nomadic Southern (or Rayleigh) Rovers side.

Opposite: The men behind the first Provincial League champions. Pictured pre-season at The Weir, l-r, are Rayleigh promoters Wally Mawdsley (left) and Pete Lansdale (centre), with the Rocket's captain, Alan Smith on the bike. (Peter Morrish/John Somerville Collection.)

There had been no action at Rayleigh in 1958 although a year later the track hosted a Cavalcade of Speed event, featuring solo racing together with sidecars and a race between a sidecar outfit and a midget car. The (extremely) mixed programme also included greyhound heats, on the flat and over hurdles and the oddest attraction of them all – a handicap race between a man (unidentified), given 450 yards to cover and an equally anonymous greyhound, given the distance of 980 yards to outpace the human runner. Research has so far failed to discover whether the winner had two or four legs!

Such events would have done little to encourage those who had looked askance at the plans for the Provincial League. But when the tapes went up on the pioneering Rayleigh-Cradley match the racing was entirely serious.

From the outset of planning for the birth of the Provincial League, Rayleigh plumped for experience. Pictured, l-r, standing, are Pete Lansdale, Reg Reeves, Eric Hockaday, Wally Mawdsley, John Leggett, Clive Hitch and Stan Stevens, with Alan Smith on the machine. Lansdale, Reeves, Smith and Hockaday had National League experience whilst Hitch and Stevens had developed successfully in the Southern Area League. (John Somerville Collection.)

Much of the focus on the birth pains of the new competition, as described in the previous chapter, focused on the North, Scotland and the Midlands. But the southern part of England was to play a major role in the establishment and the progress of the Provincial League, providing four of the initial ten member tracks, all of the top three finishers in the 1960 campaign, and the champion club for three of the competition's five seasons.

Rayleigh, given their continued existence throughout much of the 1950s, were more or less a going concern. Whilst other promotions, including Reg Fearman at Stoke were having to install a track, lighting and other equipment after many years without speedway, Weir promoters Wally Mawdsley and Pete Lansdale could concentrate their efforts on team building. As the clock ticked down during the early months of 1960, their recruitment activities had aroused considerable interest and comment in the pages of the speedway press.

Mawdsley and Lansdale's paths had crossed on many occasions throughout the 1950s. Lansdale had enjoyed an extensive career in the National League, mainly with Plymouth and Rayleigh, whilst Mawdsley's more modest career had included spells at Norwich and, coinciding with his business partner, at Plymouth and Rayleigh. At the centre of the team assembled for the PL debut at The Weir was another man who shared much of the duo's s history. Londoner Alan Smith had been a high-scoring team-mate of Lansdale at Plymouth and had two seasons in National League Division One with West Ham after the Devon track closed. He linked up again with Rayleigh for 1956 before becoming one of many riders to drift out of the sport as the bookings contracted.

When the first stirrings of revival were felt in speedway in 1959 the Lansdale and Smith partnership was briefly reunited for the first meetings of the short season of open licence racing staged by Trevor Redmond at Plymouth's Pennycross Stadium. The Rayleigh line-up, already looking strong with the combination of Smith and Lansdale and some of the pick of the Southern Area League men in the form of Eric Hockaday – whose form in the SAL had won him rides in the National League with Coventry – Stan Stevens and Clive Hitch, took on a truly formidable appearance when another veteran, Reg Reeves, with experience at Walthamstow, West Ham, Coventry, Yarmouth and Ipswich agreed to make a comeback.

Above: *Sun Street, Stoke, as the riders parade, with visitors Liverpool in the foreground. (Roy Peacock.)*

Below: *Stoke began 1960 with a side largely consisting of novices but built around the experience of promoter/rider Reg Fearman and Ray Harris. As the season progressed the team was strengthened by the addition of former Potters Ken Adams and Les Jenkins. The team pictured here features, back row, left to right, Pete Kelly, Pete Jarman, Reg Fearman, Arthur Rowe, and kneeling Gordon Owen, Les Jenkins and Ray Harris. (John Somerville Collection.)*

PL 1960 runners-up Bristol. Back row, l-r, Cliff Cox, Pat Flanagan, Ivor Toms, Ernie Baker. Front row, Roy Taylor, Johnny Hole (on machine), Ron Sharp. (John Somerville Collection.)

With three riders whose careers dated back to the late 1940s allied to some of the best talent in the SAL, Rayleigh appeared to have ignored the basis of using primarily juniors and novices, on which most other clubs were preparing for the new competition.

Was there any firm understanding, even of the gentleman's agreement nature, among the PL promoters when it came to team strengths? Reg Fearman, whose 1960 promoting interests at Stoke and particularly at Liverpool adhered to the original PL concept of encouraging the less experienced, has today a definite view, saying:

> Wally and Pete were always a little 'out of step' and did indeed flout the original intention of the Provincial League. But there was no team strength regulation in the first season although later there was to be a restriction on 'old hands' – riders who had held a full contract somewhere.

The Cradley Heath side that day at The Weir was a rather different combination to the Rockets. The Heathens' Dudley Wood Stadium in the heart of the Black Country and notorious for being difficult to find had organised a winter training school in 1959-60, run by former Heathens and Birmingham rider Phil Malpass, following the single 'pirate' meeting the previous August.

Malpass set about building a team in keeping with the PL ideal of searching for promising juniors and novices. For the opening match at Rayleigh Weir there were no experienced veterans in the Black Country side. Most of the team had appeared in the Southern Area League at some stage, with brothers Eric Eadon and Tony Eadon having raced at Brafield and for Southern Rovers, Ronnie Rolfe for Rye House, California and Ipswich, and Vic White for Ipswich. Rolfe had appeared for the Witches in National Trophy competition, when team sizes were enlarged. The rest of the side at Rayleigh, Roy Spencer, grass tracker George Bewley and Bill Coleman, were products of the Dudley Wood winter training school.

The contest, on paper, looked unbalanced and so it was to prove on the track. But before the league match began, the nearest thing to novices attached to Rayleigh took to the track for a vultures race, with the prize of the reserve slot for the Rockets at stake. Pat McKenzie, Reg Nicholls, Frank Wooster and John Leggett lined up, with McKenzie first past the finishing line to claim the team place.

Some indication of how anxious the young hopefuls considered the result of the race to be is shown by the time announced which, at seventy-nine seconds dead was faster than two of the races in the league match, on a track surface described by the visiting team as 'rough and wet'.

The actual racing, which resulted in a 50-20 win for the Rockets, was something of a let-down and must have had those who were cynical about the Provincial League congratulating themselves (prematurely as it proved) on their foresight. Eight of the 12 heats ended in maximum 5-1wins for the home side. Cradley won just two heats – Pete Lansdale fell in one of the races – and just one heat was drawn.

For Rayleigh Reg Reeves recorded a paid maximum from four rides, on three occasions following his team mate Alan Smith (nine points from three rides) over the line. Eric Hockaday scored 10 points. Stevens (9) and Hitch (8), while Lansdale's contribution was five from three starts.

It would be pleasant to record that the winner of the Vultures Race, Pat McKenzie, did well in the league match and launched a successful career in the sport. As it was, he failed to score in his first reserve ride and fell in his second. He was given two

Poole Pirates? Yes but in 1960 without the familiar skull and crossbones race jackets. When Liverpool re-opened under the name of the Pirates, the Poole management (who also promoted at Southampton) decided on a variation of the Saints colours, but blue and white rather than red stripes for the Dorset team. Pictured l-r are, standing, Ross Gilbertson, Geoff Mudge, Mick Freeman, Chum Taylor (Southampton rider acting as mechanic), and Dave Dodd. Kneeling, Gerry Bridson and Charlie Wallis. Alan Kidd on machine. (John Somerville Collection.)

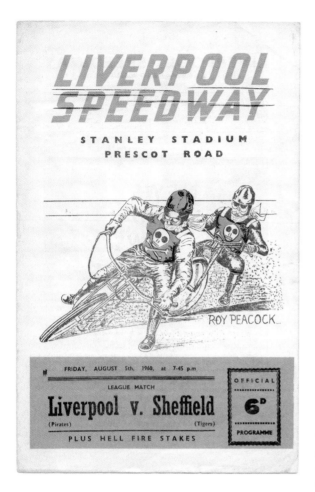

LIVERPOOL SPEEDWAY

STANLEY STADIUM
PRESCOT ROAD

ROY PEACOCK

FRIDAY, AUGUST 5th, 1960, at 7-45 p.m.

LEAGUE MATCH

Liverpool v. Sheffield

(Pirates)   (Tigers)

OFFICIAL

6ᴰ

PROGRAMME

PLUS HELL FIRE STAKES

*The Pirates of Liverpool.
(Roy Peacock.)*

more opportunities in the 1960 season but scored just one point. The other participants in the Vultures Race did little better although John Leggett was loaned to Yarmouth and made eight PL appearances, scoring 18 points plus seven bonus points.

Rayleigh, already considered by some to be too strong a side, subsequently attracted some criticism by signing another experienced rider, Roy Craighead, once of Wembley Lions, to complete their septet.

The Rayleigh-Cradley clash could hardly have been bettered as an illustration of the gulf between the juniors and the men with experience. It is easy to criticise the very different approach adopted by Rayleigh but most speedway commentators of the time supported the use of experienced riders – and as the season progressed virtually all the Provincial League sides, including Cradley, strengthened their line-ups.

Jack Rollin, surveying the Provincial League's first season in the *Speedway Star Digest*, maintained that there had been two distinct trends of thought about PL racing, 'one group considering the whole thing to be something of a Saturday afternoon run-around'. Rollin went on to say:

They were shaken to the core when they discovered that the other faction was signing up all the experienced riders that contracts could be placed in front of within the limits of decency. These experienced and often veteran riders put life into the league. Without them its measure of success would have been much smaller and it could well have failed altogether had they not been introduced.

Fortunately, as the season moved on, some of those tracks who had been in favour of juniors only changed their minds and jumped on the experience bandwagon. It made for much closer racing. Oddly enough, this swing from junior rating to experience was almost a total reversal of the original feeling current when Rayleigh first announced a strong combination, that the Rockets' strength would make a farce of the competition for the remaining nine sides.

Opposite: Harry Bastable added much-needed experience to Cradley Heath's 1960 team. (John Somerville Collection.)

The Stoke-Liverpool match run the same evening at Sun Street was somewhat closer as a contest than the proceedings at The Weir and did produce one of the first of the new league's overnight sensations in the form of a virtual novice producing a double figure score.

Although some of the bottle kiln and ironworks fires may have been damped down for the Easter Bank Holiday weekend there were still plenty of smoky chimneys around Sun Street, Hanley, to greet speedway's return to the Potteries.

At Rayleigh the attendance for the meeting against Cradley had been acceptable. The size of the crowds which began to converge on Sun Street from an early hour came as a surprise to everyone, including promoters Parker and Fearman. It was an early indication of the enthusiasm displayed by the public in most (but not quite all) of the centres staging Provincial League speedway in 1960.

The match itself, which Stoke won 44-26, was raced between two sides with a slightly better balance than had been on view at The Weir. As in Essex, there was plenty of experience on view, but with most of it in the Potters' team. By 1960 Ray Harris, a Stoke rider in two spells for eleven seasons and the holder of the club's record number of appearances in the twentieth century, was a portly character, fond of the scrumpy cider produced in such great volume in his native Herefordshire. One time Stoke junior Dingle Brown is on record as recalling that Harris brought flagons of the golden liquid to Sun Street on race nights.

Tony Robinson of fourth-place Sheffield won the PL Silver Sash by beating Doug Templeton of Edinburgh at Owlerton. After successful defences against Reg Fearman and George Hunter, he lost the Sash through injury. Placing the Sash over Robinson's head is a niece of Sheffield promoter Frank Varey (on the right). (Robinson family.)

Yarmouth Bloaters had a respectable season back in league racing, finishing seventh. The Bloater's line-up was captained by Ivor Brown, later to become a star at Cradley. Standing, l-r, are John Debbage, John Leggett (on loan from Rayleigh), John Fitzpatrick, co-promoter Ted Courtnell, Ron Bagley, Geoff Pymar and Ken Last with Ivor Brown on the machine. (John Somerville Collection.)

Whether or not cider contributed to Ray's speed around the track on its re-opening night is a matter for conjecture, but whatever the deciding factor, he scored the Provincial League's first twelve point maximum. He was the most experienced rider on display in terms of the number of matches raced, but Stoke's co-promoter, Reg Fearman had raced for Division One West Ham as a teenager in two spells in the late 1940s and early 1950s and later spent four seasons with Leicester.

For Stoke the experienced pairing of Harris and Fearman did all that was expected of them but the evening was notable for marking the start of a successful career for a novice in the Potters side, who exceeded all prior expectations.

Just behind Harris in the Stoke scorechart was the unfancied Peter Kelly, who scored ten points and was twice nursed over the line by Reg Fearman, whose tally was seven plus two bonus. Many years later Fearman, looking back at the re-opening night at Sun Street, recalled:

Peter Kelly had a few outings at Ainsdale Sands but came to Stoke straight from the Belle Vue training school. He was very quick and it was most surprising that he and a few other novices adapted so quickly to the tight bends of Sun Street. He didn't stay at Stoke for very long, returning to Belle Vue and then enjoying a good career with Bradford, Newcastle and Berwick. Peter was easy to get on with and a real racer.

The rest of the Potters side on the night had eked out an existence during the 1950s riding at training schools, in second halves and getting scarce competitive rides on the few open licence tracks that operated in the north and midlands and, of course, in the Parker-organised 'pirate' meetings and Cavalcade of Sport events. One Stoke rider, Ted Connor, deserves recognition as one of the founding fathers of the Provincial League for the vital role he had played in persuading Northern juniors to become legitimate.

Liverpool were held together on the night by Brian Craven, the elder brother of Belle Vue star and 1954 World Champion Peter. Brian, who scored 12 points from five rides – nearly half his team's total – was by far the most experienced Liverpool rider on the night, had begun his speedway career at Liverpool, his home town team, in 1950, later taking advantage of relatively limited opportunities with the Aces at Hyde Road.

He enjoyed a substantial run in Belle Vue's National League side in 1956, with the highlight being a nine points tally from reserve in a crushing Aces National Trophy victory over a weak Birmingham side. With competition for rides in the late 1950s so intense, Brian Craven was one of the many who retired to concentrate on career (in his case as a skilled engineer), only to be tempted back to the sport by the creation of the Provincial League.

Craven's only real support at Stoke came from northern junior Roy Peacock, a product of the training schools at Ainsdale and Newton Heath. Peacock scored a creditable six points (paid seven).

After the closure of Liverpool at the end of the 1960 season, Brian Craven moved to Stoke and later became part of the Provincial League inspired revival at Newcastle.

As the season progressed the other tracks followed the lead of Rayleigh and Stoke in opening their doors. Cradley introduced PL racing to the Dudley Wood fans on 16 April, the day after the meetings at The Weir and Sun Street and Liverpool were in action at Stanley Stadium on Easter Monday. Sheffield and Bristol opened for business on 6 May, at Owlerton and Knowle Stadium respectively, and Edinburgh staged the first PL meeting

Edinburgh Monarchs had a moderate season as far as results were concerned, with just five league wins. This record had little effect upon the crowds at Old Meadowbank, some of the best in Britain. (Peter Colvin.)

The Monarchs team line-up pictured here includes former Australian test star and New Cross rider Ron Johnnie (second left). When Johnnie Hoskins re-opened New Cross in 1960 Johnson, who had suffered serious injuries during his career, attempted a comeback at the age of fifty-three. Johnnie sent him to Scotland (where Johnson was born in 1907) and he rode in six matches for Edinburgh, but only scored a single point. (John Somerville Collection.)

in Scotland the following day. There was then a substantial gap before the final three members of the new league made their home debuts – Bradford on 4 June, Yarmouth on 21 June and Poole on 29 June.

It soon became apparent that the league table was to be effectively divided into three groups. Rayleigh was not the only club to track an experienced line-up virtually from the start, although in one or two cases the Rockets' early performances prompted rival promotions to smartly open the cheque book.

Poole, pushed Rayleigh hard all season and the Pirates' results were identical to the Rockets – in each case the 18 PL matches produced 16 wins and two defeats. Rayleigh were awarded the title on the strength of having more race points. The Dorset team, like Rayleigh, had been among the selected group of tracks managing to operate for most of the slump years.

SAL product Ross Gilbertson topped the Pirates' averages in 1960 just ahead of Ken Middleditch and Australian Geoff Mudge and Alan Kidd were solid scorers.

Third placed Bristol, two match points behind Rayleigh and Poole, were the final members of the leading group in the league table and like their main rivals had considerable experience in their squad from the outset. Johnny Hole had been a regular member of the Bulldogs team before its relegation from the top flight at the end of the 1953 season and made a major contribution to Bristol's Division Two championship side in 1954, especially on his home track. Two other members of the 1960 PL team, Cliff Cox and Roy Taylor had also made appearances for the Bulldogs in National League Division Two racing before Bristol withdrew midseason in 1955.

The Bulldogs caused a shock in their very first Provincial League match when they travelled to Rayleigh on 29 April 1960 and beat the Rockets (who were minus top scorer Alan Smith) 37-35. A week later Rayleigh were again their opponents, at Knowle, and on this occasion the Rockets, with Smith scoring a faultless 12pt maximum, ran out winners by 38 points to 34.

Despite a crushing home victory over Bradford the Bristol management decided the side needed strengthening if it was to mount a real challenge for the first PL title. Into the side came the vastly experienced Trevor Redmond, formerly of Wembley Lions and, more recently, Swindon Robins. Redmond, who for a couple of seasons in the late '50s had concentrated on his open licence promoting interests at St Austell, was to prove a major asset to Bristol, scoring more than 200 points at an average of 10 a match, finishing second in the end of season scorechart just behind Hole, another ten point man.

The second grouping to emerge in the infant Provincial League consisted of five teams that could more or less hold their own in the centre of the table: Sheffield, Stoke, Cradley Heath, Yarmouth and Edinburgh.

Sheffield, where league speedway had been absent for a decade honoured to a substantial degree the intention to give opportunities to relatively inexperienced Northern riders such as Malcolm Bruce and Stuart Hickman, together with the young Australian Derrol Melbin, a clear favourite with the Owlerton crowd, despite his relative lack of points. Jack Winstanley and Len Williams (who only rode in home matches) brought considerable experience but the Tigers' real strength came from their loanees from Belle Vue, Tony Robinson and Jack Kitchen, who rattled up 300 points between them

Stoke, as the season progressed, introduced more former Sun Street favourites into their side, notably Les Jenkins and Ken Adams, who provided significant back-up to top-scorers Harris and Fearman. No fewer than 17 riders donned the Potters colours in PL racing, including another rider in Pete Jarman who was to become a firm Sun Street favourite, and the future Wolverhampton co-promoter Bill Bridgett. John Hart, son of the one-time Birmingham favourite Phil 'Tiger' Hart made his competitive debut, scoring a single point in his only league appearance.

Hoping for a return to the spotlight in 1960. Ron Johnson pictured in his speedway heyday, at New Cross Stadium, the scene of his greatest triumphs. (Author's Collection.)

The Liverpool Pirates towards the end of the 1960 PL season, when the team had been strengthened by Belle Vue rider Bryce Subritzky and veteran Wal Morton. Pictured, l-r standing, Dennis Jenkins, Graham Beattie, Dave Dodd, Wal Morton, Col Smith. On machine is Bryce Subritzky and kneeling is Derek Skyner. (John Somerville Collection.)

Of the middle group of teams Cradley Heath, Rayleigh's first opponents, had stuck closest to the junior and novice principle whilst achieving reasonable success on the track. The Heathens' early programme comprised home and away matches (both ending in defeat against Rayleigh) and a home draw against Bristol, before getting some relief from home victories over Bradford, Poole and Stoke.

The Dudley Wood outfit's improved form came without any substantial change in the side as former Southern Area League men Rolfe, Eadon and White (mentioned earlier in the chapter) scored consistently. It was not until June that Cradley strengthened the team to any degree, making an inspired signing in Harry Bastable, who stepped down from National League Leicester, reputedly for a transfer fee of £50!

Birmingham-born Bastable had started his career with the Heathens and spent three seasons (1950-52) at Dudley Wood. He joined Birmingham in 1953 and had five seasons with the Brummies in speedway's top tier, until the track closed mid-season in 1957, when he linked up with Leicester. His second spell at Cradley lasted for all five of the Provincial League's seasons, and he rode in 16 British League matches in 1965.

The East of England has traditionally been a hotbed for speedway and the fourth of the middle group of tracks in the initial Provincial League season, Yarmouth, enjoyed two years (1948-49) in the National League Division Three and four in Division Two before calling it a day at the end of the 1953 campaign. Subsequently the Bloaters, renowned for the unusual shape of their track at Caister Road in the east coast holiday resort, had something of a chequered career.

The track operated under an open licence in 1957 and 1958, staging challenge matches and individual events during the peak holiday months only, using a mix of National League stars, including Peter Craven, Ove Fundin and Barry Briggs, and some Southern Area League juniors. Although the mix was at first similar for 1958, there were more opportunities for junior riders and amongst those introduced to the Caister Road set up was Leicester junior Ivor Brown, who was to prove the dominant rider when the Bloaters moved first into the Southern Area League (for 1959) and then into the PL in 1960.

Yarmouth, the only Southern Area League side to be successful in their application to join the Provincial League tracked what had been the basis of their SAL line-up, with Brown, John Fitzpatrick, John Debbage, Ken Last, Anthony Childs and Ron Bagley. Experience was added in the shape of the veteran Geoff Pymar and the Bloaters had a respectable season, winning seven matches.

Edinburgh, the only Scottish contenders in 1960 hovered between the middle and bottom groups of clubs.

Despite winning just five of their 18 league fixtures, the Monarchs were arguably the most interesting club in the new competition and probably the best supported. Ian

Hoskins had remained in Scotland after the sport's collapse, taking a job in industry and dabbling with speedway at Motherwell.

The Motherwell venture had revealed to Hoskins that there was a nucleus of Scottish riders keen to continue in the sport, although deprived of opportunities to race on a regular basis. During the 1960 season Edinburgh effectively used just nine riders – the smallest squad in the competition. Seven were Scots – farming brothers Doug and Willie Templeton, Jimmy Tannock, Jimmy Cox, Gordon Mitchell George Hunter (a discovery from the open licence season at Motherwell) and speedway legend Ron Johnson, a test match star with Australia but actually born in Duntocher, Dunbartonshire, Scotland.

The squad was completed by two Englishmen, Fred Greenwell, who although a native of the north-east of England had ridden in the 1950s for Rayleigh and Southern Rovers, and Reg Luckhurst a junior from Ashford in Kent. The Templeton brothers, Tannock and Cox had started racing speedway early enough to have featured in the team line-ups of the Scottish league sides of the early 1950s.

Although the Templetons and Tannock are better remembered today, Cox was actually the most experienced of the group of riders Ian Hoskins put together for the Provincial League, having made more than 120 starts for the Monarchs during the four seasons 1951-54. He was an enigma throughout his career at Old Meadowbank, mostly only picking up the odd point or two, but capable of occasionally scoring eight or nine,

Ron Johnson was fifty-three years of age when he turned up at Old Meadowbank in the spring of 1960. Once the idol of the New Cross fans, a National League title and London Cup winner with the Old Kent Road team, his career had effectively ended in a spectacular crash at Wimbledon in 1949. He refused to accept defeat and had made an earlier comeback attempt at Glasgow Ashfield in 1952, but could only score 35 points in 16 appearances.

His Old Meadowbank adventure in 1960 was even more humiliating for one of the greats of the sport. He rode in six matches, scoring one point and one bonus. Ian Hoskins, in his fascinating autobiography *History of the Speedway Hoskins* (First Edition Publishers,New Zealand ISBN 1-877391387) explained:

> I was foolish in letting him ride. His timing had gone. He knew what to do but was always a fraction too late in opening his throttle. It was heartbreaking to see him. He wisely retired at the end of the season.

The final sub-section of the 1960 Provincial League table comprised the bottom two clubs, Liverpool, who won four matches over the course of the season, and Bradford, who managed just one victory.

Both tracks had operated 'pirate' meetings in 1959. Liverpool, on the opening night at Stoke in 1960 (described in more detail at the start of this chapter) tracked six of the men who had appeared in the final match of the previous season. The only change in the line-up was the inclusion of Brian Craven, in place of Arthur Rowe, who switched to the other Mike Parker/Reg Fearman track at Stoke.

Sadly for the Liverpool fans, Craven was injured in May after shaping to be one of the new league's top performers. He did not re-appear until the middle of August and immediately reproduced his early season form.

Liverpool used more than 20 riders during the course of the season, with few if any of their novice riders making any real impact. It is interesting in the light of Ron Johnson's failed comeback at Edinburgh to note that one of the many riders introduced to try and strengthen the 1960 Liverpool team as the weeks went by was another veteran in his fifties.

Wal Morton enjoyed a speedway career less stellar perhaps than Ron Johnson's, but with fewer injury problems. And in complete contrast to Johnson's Edinburgh experience, Wal was to ride regularly in the Provincial League's first four seasons at Liverpool, Middlesbrough, Bradford, and Hackney, and also raced – as an official OAP – in a couple of matches in 1964 in the Metropolitan League.

Parker and Fearman introduced extra experience into the Liverpool camp at intervals. As in the case of Sheffield, Belle Vue were only too glad to loan out riders from the impressive ranks of their junior strength. Bryce Subritzky and Dennis Jenkins from Hyde Road stiffened the side and scored nearly 140 points between them. Another Belle Vue

Bottom spot in the initial Provincial League, with just one victory in 18 matches, went to Bradford. The team lined up at Odsal as follows: Back row, Jess Halliday (promoter), Stan Holey, Vic Lonsdale, Roy Challoner, Eddie Rigg (team manager). Kneeling, Norman Redmond (left) and Tommy Roper. Ray Day on machine. (John Somerville Collection.)

junior, Jim Yacobi, raced in one match for the Merseysiders and showed his potential, scoring nine points. At the end of the season Wal Morton was the leading scorer for Liverpool, with 115 points from his 13 matches. Brian Craven totalled 99 from his nine matches and Subritzky was also a ten-point man, with 93 points from nine appearances.

A Liverpool team with Morton, a fit Craven, Subritzky and some steady second strings might have achieved much better than the team's eventual placing next to the bottom of the league.

The bottom spot was occupied by Bradford, where promoter Jess Halliday had brought speedway back to the gigantic Odsal Stadium in the shape of the 1959 'pirate' meetings. Like Liverpool, Bradford started off with a side which on paper looked somewhat stronger than the group of riders who had competed the previous year but the Panthers, as they were re-named for their PL debut lost eleven straight league and knock out cup matches home and away between 30 April and 23 July.

Their one and only victory in the league came on the latter date when the visitors to Odsal were Edinburgh, including Ron Johnson at reserve. For the home side Ray Day, Tommy Roper and Belle Vue loanee Jim Yacobi (riding for his second PL club) were consistent but the home hero was Vic Lonsdale, who had dropped down to reserve for the match and scored eleven points. In a narrow encounter, with Doug Templeton top-scoring for the visitors with ten points, Bradford won 37-34.

Many of the Yorkshire team's defeats, both away from home and at Odsal, were by heavy margins. Bradford suffered a complete whitewash at Rayleigh in mid-August, taking just twelve points from the twelve heats in reply to the Rockets' 59. The ultimate embarrassment could have been avoided if Bradford could have got a man across the line in the penultimate heat, but both their riders failed to finish. Ray Day and Stan Holey with four points apiece headed the Bradford scorechart.

As is not unusual where speedway racing is concerned, there were some odd results. Rayleigh beat Poole at The Weir and the Pirates reversed the result in Dorset, although the Rockets perhaps deserved the overall bragging rights with a two point victory over Poole in the knock out Cup at Wimborne Road.

In addition to the league match fare the Provincial League launched its own knock-out cup competition, which was hailed as a 'big success' by the sport's media. The competition began at the end of May with one-off matches and ended in September with a two-legged final. Bristol, third in the league behind Rayleigh and Poole, gained a measure of revenge by defeating the Rockets in the final.

Throughout the competition the one-off format produced some heavy defeats for the weaker teams. Bristol won 61-35 at Bradford and Stoke defeated Cradley 60-35 at Sun Street. Rayleigh won 49-47 at Poole in the third road whilst In the semi-finals Bristol travelled to Scotland and beat Edinburgh 58-38 and the Rockets gained a 52-43 success against Stoke, despite fifteen points from Reg Fearman. Rayleigh staged the first leg of the final, winning 52-41 at The Weir to take an eleven point lead to Knowle and given their league form and on the evidence of their earlier cup win at Poole, were fancied to lift the trophy.

Bristol's heat leader trio proved far too strong in the event, with the Provincial League's undoubted man of the season Trevor Redmond registering an 18 point maximum, supported not only by Cliff Cox with 14 points and Johnny Hole with 13, but also by second strings Pat Flanagan (eight points) and Chris Julian (five). The deficit was quickly wiped out and the Bulldogs went on to establish their own eleven point advantage overall.

The initial Provincial League Riders' Championship final was held at Cradley Heath and won by Bristol's Trevor Redmond (right), with a 15 point maximum. Ken Middleditch of Poole (centre) beat Eric Hockaday of Rayleigh (left) in a run-off for second place. (Peter Morrish/John Somerville Collection.)

In the individual event area Redmond again took the honours. For the initial Provincial League Riders' Championship final the method of qualification was not entirely satisfactory, with five of the ten tracks preferring to nominate riders rather than stage a qualifying round. In the event, the top three scorers in the Final at Cradley – Redmond, Ken Middleditch and Eric Hockaday had all booked their places by qualifying with impressive scores in their rounds.

The PL also followed the lead of the Southern Area League and introduced a Silver Sash match race competition. To emphasise his status as man of the season, Trevor Redmond was the man in possession at the end of the campaign.

The Provincial League tracks, with the exception of Yarmouth, also staged World Championship Qualifying rounds. The Norfolk track, depending as ever on support from holidaymakers, operated from 21 June to 6 September. The Bloaters' riders did compete in the World Championship rounds and top man Ivor Brown, despite lacking a home track meeting, qualified for the next round.

A number of National League second strings competed in the PL round and the 20 qualifiers for Round Two comprised 11 NL riders and nine from the Provincial teams. Dennis Newton of Norwich was the unbeaten top scorer, with 15 point maximums at Sheffield and Poole, with Reg Reeves of Rayleigh and Reg Fearman of Stoke not far behind on 28 and 26 points respectively.

In Round Two itself, matched against the finest riders in the sport, the PL men found it heavy going and none progressed any further.

The first season of the Provincial League also produced one of the most ironical situations in the often incredible history of the sport. At least six of the ten tracks attracted good attendances but as journalist Jack Rollin, reviewing the new league's debut season for the *Speedway Star* Digest commented:

> Success was no yardstick. Even Bradford, with a solitary success, had a better average gate than champions Rayleigh.

Six of Rayleigh's nine league fixtures at The Weir produced winning margins of 47, 44, 36, 30, 30 and 26 points. Rayleigh owed their winning title to the race points they piled up – 808 to Poole's 721 – but it proved to be fatal to attendances.

There was plenty of open licence racing in 1960, all adding to the belief that speedway's future was much brighter than it had been just a couple of years earlier. Tracks operating outside the National and Provincial Leagues included Rye House, Eastbourne and Aldershot, excluded by Control Board ruling from the PL itself, whilst Exeter and Plymouth made cases for inclusion in the new league in 1961.

Wigan also ran on an open licence but by far the most interesting development outside the league structure was a new promotion at the Alexander Sports Stadium, Birmingham, where former Brummie favourite Phil 'Tiger' Hart joined forces with Doug Ellis, later better known as the controversial chairman of Aston Villa Football Club, to bring speedway back to the Second City.

Birmingham used National League riders for the challenge matches and individual events at Perry Barr but an application to the PL seemed on the cards for 1961. Any plans were scuppered when the owners of the stadium, the Birchfield Harriers Athletic Club decided that speedway was no longer welcome. The last rider to complete a circuit of the historic venue before the track was torn up was John Hart, son of Phil 'Tiger Hart'. John had made his Provincial League debut at Stoke and went on to a distinguished career with Cradley, Leicester, Sheffield and, eventually, with Birmingham.

Speedway in Birmingham was revived in the 1970s at the greyhound stadium close by the Alexander Sports Stadium and Hart at last became a fully-fledged Brummie. Speedway in Birmingham has a complicated past and the current Perry Bar Greyhound Stadium, although on the site of the Alexander Stadium as it existed in 1960, is a new development with a new track. The greyhound stadium where the 1970s Brummies raced is now a shopping centre.

Chapter 8

1961: HELLO AND GOODBYE AS TRACKS COME AND GO

IN the early months of 1960 speedway pundits had been split firmly down the middle when it came to their predictions about the likely fate of the Provincial League. Twelve months later, as the new competition prepared for a second season, both the enthusiasts and the sceptics could find something to justify their earlier beliefs.

Most of the ten tracks which started and, more importantly, finished the 1960 season reported good and in some cases excellent crowd figures. The speedway public, particularly in those parts of the country which had not seen league racing for many years, took to the unpredictable nature of the racing and the showmanship of the new promoters.

But whilst those who had backed the PL from the start rejoiced in its success, those who had predicted doom, gloom and disaster felt themselves to be at least partly justified in their scepticism when four out of the ten founder tracks failed to show up again for 1961. To lose forty per cent of your membership said very little, they claimed, for the stability of the new competition.

Facing down the doomsayers from an early stage had been speedway columnist Jack Rollin, whose main fear (as recorded in Chapter Seven) had been what would have happened to the PL at the outset if the promoters who plumped initially for sides made of juniors and novices had not brought in more experienced and crowd-pleasing recruits as the campaign progressed. Now, as a new season dawned, Rollin added:

> Few gave the new-born league much chance to live, in a speedway world which had seen only the fittest survive. By all reasonable thinking, it should have met its end within a year of first seeing daylight. But now its future looks much healthier than the one facing its elder brother [the National League].

Rollin believed the PL promoters had relied for success on two main points of appeal – the fact that the majority of the 1960 tracks were in areas in which speedway had been

A West Country goodbye. Bristol's Knowle Stadium, pictured in its National League glory days, was sold for £125,000, closed at the end of January 1961, and was demolished and replaced by housing.

absent for some years, whilst the second factor was the fairly quick realisation that 'names' attracted fans and that, as Jack Rollin expressed it, 'one personality proved worth half a dozen wholehearted novices'.

Despite the general aura of success hanging over the PL, its promoters nevertheless had hurdles to cross in the winter of 1960-61. The withdrawal of Liverpool and Bradford was no great surprise, considering their lack of success in the first season, but the PL's first major blow to its prestige was the closure of Bristol.

To secure a venue with a National League Division One pedigree in one of England's major cities had been a feather in the cap for the PL. Sadly, Knowle Stadium became a relatively early casualty of a new disease – the urge to re-develop valuable sites for new and more profitable purposes. As this urge coincided with a decline in the post-war popularity of an evening 'at the dogs', the next few decades were to spell the end for greyhound stadia large and small across Britain.

When speedway first began in 1928 it settled comfortably into the large and usually well-appointed arenas that had been constructed for dog racing following its introduction from the United States in 1926. The problem that later had to be faced was the fact that so many of these stadia, in both London and the provinces, offered tasty locations for the property development boom of the second half of the twentieth century.

Knowle, opened in 1927 to an 8000 attendance, was sold for £125,000, with the final meeting taking place on 28 January 1961. The stadium was quickly demolished, to be replaced by housing, with one of the streets which sprang up on the site named Long Eaton Drive. No connection between Bristol and the Derbyshire one-time speedway centre can be discovered by the author.

Greyhound racing continued at the city's other track, Eastville Stadium, the home of Bristol Rovers Football Club, which would be the location for Bristol's 1970s speedway revival. When Newport shifted their base across the Severn Bridge, racing took place in front of large attendances, ironically enough on a track laid each week on top of the greyhound circuit and dug up at the end of the meeting.

Bradford, rock bottom of the PL in 1960 and Liverpool, who were next to bottom, also closed their doors at the end of the season. In the case of Bradford the closure was

Above: *Plymouth Bulldogs 1961. Standing, l-r, Chris Blewett, Frank Johnson, Ray Wickett, Jack Scott, Pat Flanagan, Ron Bagley, Chris Julian. Cliff Cox on machine. (John Somerville Collection.)*

Below: *The ups and downs in the West of England continued when Exeter joined the Provincial League for 1961. The County Ground had last seen National League Division Two racing in 1955 but operated on an open licence in 1957. The stadium was owned by Exeter Chiefs Rugby Union club and the greyhound track was one of the few examples placed inside rather than outside the speedway circuit. (John Somerville Collection.)*

Exeter were promoted by the Rayleigh duo of Wally Mawdsley and Pete Lansdale. Pictured is the 1961 team, back row l-r, Francis Cann, Billie Smith, Wally Mawdsley, Eric Howe, Eric Hockaday. Front row, l-r, Len Silver, Pete Lansdale, Clive Hitch. (John Somerville Collection.)

temporary but speedway was never again to be seen in Liverpool. The fourth casualty was Yarmouth, a coastal resort track which, for most of its life, flourished only during the peak holiday season.

What saved the day, cheered the PL's management committee and took much of the wind out of the sails of the sceptics was the fact that the competition had no trouble whatsoever in replacing the departing tracks. There were revivals for 1961 in the North East, with the re-opening (in each case after many years) of Newcastle and Middlesbrough, in the West Country, where Plymouth and Exeter returned to league racing, and in the Midlands, where Monmore Green, Wolverhampton saw speedway for the first time in seven years.

Despite the loss of Bristol, West Country fans had plenty of local derby matches to enjoy. Pictured here is heat two of Plymouth's 40-38 home victory over Poole Pirates on 21 April 1961, as Cliff Cox of the Bulldogs (on the outside line) prepares to overtake Poole's Ross Gilbertson. (Peter Morrish/John Somerville Collection.)

The position as the tapes went up for the 1961 season was an eleven-track Provincial League, a net gain of one venue compared to the first season.

Bristol had quickly found a new home at Plymouth's Pennycross Stadium and the Bulldogs nickname moved west with the riders. With Exeter also returning to league fray it meant a return to Devon derbies and Cornish neighbours St Austell, an open licence track, also benefited from the South West Peninsula boom, racing with their neighbours in a subsidiary competition, the Western Cup.

Exeter were promoted by Wally Mawdsley and Pete Lansdale, who had been the management team behind 1960 PL champions Rayleigh, Despite the on-track success at the Essex centre, the crowds were poor and Mawdsley and Lansdale were looking for Exeter to boost their speedway business. The duo split the successful Rayleigh side between the two centres, with Lansdale himself, Clive Hitch and Eric Hockday from the Rockets' team transferring to Exeter, whilst Billie Smith, brother of Rayleigh's 1960 top man Alan, also moved west.

Northern Speedways Ltd, the company formed by Mike Parker and Reg Fearman, opened the three other 1961 newcomers. Reg Fearman operated Stoke (as in 1960) and Middlesbrough, whilst Parker was the leading figure at Newcastle and Wolverhampton, where he was assisted by former rider Bill Bridgett.

Journalist Jack Rollin was again given the task of reviewing the Provincial League at the end of the 1961 campaign. This time he commented on the 'growing confidence' of the new competition, which had come as a surprise to those who had tended to write it off from the start. Rollin said:

> The principle of the Provincial League is one that will probably last. The league has no false illusions of grandeur and is striving to appeal with the best entertainment it is capable of producing.

The 1961 PL action moves north to Sheffield. Former Tigers' rider Guy Allott got the move he wanted back to Owlerton Stadium after spending four years at National League Leicester. He is seen practising starts, waved off by Sheffield promoter Frank Varey. (John Somerville Collection.)

Smart casual in the Sheffield pits for two of the Tigers' star men of the Provincial League period, Clive Featherby (left) and Guy Allott. (Ivan Stephenson/John Somerville Collection.)

The promoters had been keen to introduce the principle of early season area competitions, introducing a greater element of competition to the warm-up to the Provincial League proper. The concept got under way with a Northern League, with seven of the eleven PL members from Edinburgh, the North of England and the Midlands competing.

In the event, the number of participating teams was too many for a contest designed to be run over a limited time period and many of the matches ended up being raced for both PL and Northern League points. Nevertheless, the idea was voted a success in principle and, suitably adapted, lasted for the rest of the Provincial League's existence. Stoke won the competition ahead of runners-up Edinburgh, whilst Newcastle were the wooden spoonists

The PL Knock-out Cup had been one of the most welcome innovations of the league's first season and there was more acclaim for the competition in 1961, when Cradley Heath defeated Edinburgh 102 points to 87 on aggregate.

The Monarchs were drawn at home to Plymouth in the one-off semi-finals and the visitors had no reward for their marathon trip across the border, losing 55-40 to the home side. Wayne Briggs top-scored for Edinburgh with 12 points from his five rides and there was solid support from all other members of the team. Maury Mattingley (13) and Cliff Cox (11) were best for the West Country outfit.

Cradley Heath's route to the final was via a 55-41 home win over Poole, thanks to a 15 point maximum from Ivor Brown and 12 points from Harry Bastable. Geoff Mudge (14), Ross Gilbertson (13) and Tony Lewis (8) scored all but six of the Pirates' points.

Early season challenge match action at Owlerton in April 1961 as Derek Timms is seen on the inside line leading home favourite Tony Robinson. Cradley won 50-28. (Robinson family.)

Further north still to Middlesbrough, newcomers to the 1961 Provincial League after thirteen years without league racing at Cleveland Park. The Bears' team is pictured, standing l-r, Eric Boothroyd, Don Wilkinson, Rick France, Vic Lonsdale, Tommy Roper. Geoff Pymar on machine and Fred Greenwell kneeling. (John Somerville Collection.)

Continuing the journey north to Newcastle, also making their debut in the Provincial League in 1961 after a decade of closure. The Newcastle St John Ambulance men seem to think visiting Wolverhampton rider Ernie Lessitter's bent front wheel is amusing, but Ernie, who fell in the final heat of the match after collecting eight points (two wins) from his first three rides does not share the joke. Wolves won the match 40-37. (Spencer Oliver/ John Somerville Collection.)

Cradley staged the first leg of the final at Dudley Wood and the Heathens' crushing 68-28 victory left the Monarchs with little hope of pulling back such a large deficit. For Cradley Ivor Brown scored a faultless 15 point maximum, both Harry Bastable and Derek Timms were unbeaten by opponents and were paid for 15 points and Ivor Davies (10 points) also reached double figures.

Edinburgh won just one heat, Doug Templeton top scored with nine points and brother Willie was the Monarchs only heat winner. At Old Meadowbank Monarchs pulled back the intimidating 40-point deficit to just 15 points overall, winning the second leg 59-34. Dick Campbell was top scorer with a paid 15 point maximum and Jimmy Tannock notched up three wins in a ten point haul. On this occasion it was Cradley struggling to have riders first past the post, with just Derek Timms and reserve Tony Eadon taking the chequered flag.

Opposite: Eric Boothroyd of Middlesbrough and Doug Templeton of Edinburgh toss for gate positions before a match at Cleveland Park. (Spencer Oliver/John Somerville Collection.)

On the Northern Riders' Championship podium in 1961, winner Tony Robinson (left) of Sheffield and Gil Goldfinch of Newcastle. (Robinson family.)

In the individual sphere PL riders again competed in the 1961 World Championship with qualifying rounds at all member tracks except Newcastle. Poole's Tony Lewis was the most successful PL entrant, making it through to the semi-final round.

The PL hosted three 'tests' against the National League in 1961, at Stoke, Wolverhampton and Newcastle, with the junior competition winning two of the matches to take the series, against a not-over strong NL side, lacking any stars.

For the 1961 Provincial Riders' Championship all eleven tracks staged qualifying rounds and the final was held in London, at former National League glamour venue Harringay, where Reg Reeves was the winner with a 15 point maximum.

Both Reeves and the previous year's victor, Trevor Redmond were unbeaten in four heats when they met in heat 17. Redmond, forced to change tracks when Bristol closed at the end of 1960, had only ridden in the PL for part of the season and had been seeded into the Harringay final as the reigning champion. His chance of retaining his title disappeared when a chain broke but he had the consolation of beating Maury Mattingley, who had also finished with 12 points, in a run-off for second place.

Redmond had been the last man to hold the Silver Sash in 1960, but was not eligible to defend his title at the start of 1961, having not yet linked up with new track Wolverhampton at that stage. The first Sash contest of the year was at Middlesbrough on 6 April, when Bears' Rick France beat Sheffield's Stuart Hickman, who scored a 12 point maximum as the Tigers won the league match 42-36 – twice as many points as France had managed.

The two outstanding riders in the competition in 1961 were Ivor Brown of Cradley and Eric Boothroyd of Middlesbrough, who both held the title through four challenges.

Chapter 9
1962: POOLE MAKE IT A PROVINCIAL LEAGUE DOUBLE

THE Provincial League's third season brought another increase in its membership, coinciding with a slump in the strength of the senior National League. Thirteen tracks, two more than in 1961 and the largest starting membership so far, began the PL season and thirteen managed to complete their fixtures.

The National League started out with eight teams, three fewer than in the previous campaign and then lost Ipswich in mid-season. It was the first mid-term closure the NL had suffered since it had become one big league for 1957, but on that occasion Birmingham's withdrawal was amply compensated by Bradford stepping in to take over their fixtures. In its first two seasons the PL, despite resignations during the close seasons, had not experienced a mid-season closure, a position it was to maintain in 1962.

There was, almost as a matter of course, a considerable change in the composition of the Provincial League. It was a pattern which had emerged at the end of the competition's first season and was to continue throughout the five campaigns of the PL's existence.

For 1962 there was just one winter casualty, with Rayleigh bowing out. On the other side of the coin there were three newcomers in the shape of the league's first Welsh club, Neath, the return of founder member Bradford (at Greenfield Greyhound Stadium rather than at Odsal) and the generally welcomed addition of Leicester, with the Hunters stepping down from the National League after a slump in attendances at Blackbird Road.

Trevor Redmond, a Bristol rider in 1960, did not join several other Bulldogs riders when the promotion transferred to Plymouth in 1961. He continued to promote and ride at non-league St Austell and at Shelbourne Park in Dublin, and had a brief but successful

The Provincial League's claim to be a truly national competition was fully justified with the arrival in 1962 of its first Welsh team, the Neath Dragons. Pictured, back row, l-r, are: Brian Leamon, Glyn Chandler, Mike Erskine, Roy Taylor, Howdy Cornell. Front kneeling, l-r, George Major, Fred Powell, Jon Erskine, Ken Williams. (Sally Chandler.)

Conversation piece between riders from two of the Provincial League's newcomers in 1962. Neath riders Roy Taylor (left) and Glyn Chandler are pictured with Leicester's Harry Edwards in the pits at the Welsh track. Edwards survived a Japanese prisoner of war camp to ride speedway for several tracks. (Sally Chandler.)

late season spell at injury-hit Wolverhampton. In his first appearance at Monmore his seven points helped Wolves to a welcome 41-37 victory over Black Country rivals Cradley.

For 1962 he was back full-time in the PL, re-introducing the sport to Wales for the first time since the closure of Cardiff (Penarth Road) at the end of 1953. Redmond discovered the existence of the Abbey Stadium in Neath, which took its name from the fact that it was overlooked by the ruins of a Cistercian Monastery, once the largest in the Principality. Stock car racing took place in 1955 but was short lived, after crowds quickly declined.

Redmond used the safety fence and other equipment from Cardiff. The track was initially reported as having a surface of fine slag but rider Glyn Chandler, who was part of the Neath Welsh Dragons team, believed it was mixed in with coal dust, as he, his team-mates and the opposition looked like coal miners at the end of a meeting.

Neath were a great success on the track, finishing second in the PL largely due to the contributions of Redmond himself, Chandler, and the unknown Jon Erskine and Australian Charlie Monk. The *Five Star Speedway Annual* rated Neath as *the* team of 1962 and enthused:

> Trevor Redmond created something out of nothing, put a team without stars on a strange new track, rode with them, captained them, team-managed them and kidded them that they were doing fine.

Off the track however, little went right for the Welsh venture. The Abbey Stadium had no covered accommodation for poor weather and there was an epidemic in the town which discouraged people from gathering in crowds. Towards the end of the season four Provincial League matches were staged at the sister track, St Austell, and that was the last of speedway in Neath.

Neath today is notorious to speedway historians and collectors of memorabilia for the rarity of items, particularly photographs of action at the venue. More exists for stock car racing, with photographs on the Stoxnet website. There is also some footage of stock car racing at the Abbey Stadium, available to watch free of charge on the British Film Institute (BFI) site. This material shows the rough and ready nature of the set-up, together with a glimpse of typical South Wales Valleys landscapes.

If Neath is a tale of almost heroic success in terms of racing and endeavour, but ultimate commercial failure, the story of Leicester is one of simple tragedy. Opened under the banner of the Parker/Fearman combine, the Hunters had previously operated in the National League as part of the Midland Sports Stadium interest and a sister track to Coventry, under millionaire Alan Sanderson and Charles Ochiltree.

The author feels a special attachment to 1962, Neath and Leicester. His first ever speedway meeting, a Provincial League Riders Championship Round at Exeter in August included two Neath riders, Jon Erskine and South African Howdy Cornell, and their colourful Welsh Dragons body colours made an impression. A little later, in September, he watched his first league match, Leicester v Neath.

The Exeter meeting had taken place on a sunny summer evening, with a holiday atmosphere at the County Ground. At Leicester the light was failing at the start of the meeting and although the entrance close to the grandstand – which had been described earlier by World Champion Jack Young as having an ambience similar to a super cinema – was impressive the high terracing all around Blackbird Road, virtually empty that night, made the overall atmosphere one of gloom.

Ochiltree and Sanderson had closed Leicester when the average attendance went down to around 3000 people. Parker and Fearman were lucky to get more than 1000 spectators through the gates.

Coincidentally, the author's third meeting (and start of regular speedway watching) was Long Eaton v St Austell, the first meeting at the Derbyshire track when it re-opened in 1963, which featured Redmond and the bulk of his 1962 Neath team for St Austell and, for the Archers, Monk and Erskine (ex-Welsh Dragons) and Slant Payling and Vic White from the Leicester side of the year before.

Leicester suffered in 1962 from riders, particularly Eric Hockaday, being switched between tracks. The Hunters' greatest achievement was the discovery of the aptly named Norman Hunter. A season of open licence events in 1963 featuring National League riders run by Sanderson and Ochiltree was also a failure. It was ironic that when Reg Fearman and Ron Wilson transferred the Long Eaton team and licence to Blackbird Road in 1968, the crowds flocked back in large numbers after the fallow period.

The third 1962 newcomer to the PL, a revived Bradford racing at Greenfields, also endured lack of success. The well-appointed greyhound stadium needed a much smaller crowd than Odsal to create an atmosphere but crowds follow a winning team. Bradford's

Very far removed from the ramshackle surroundings of Neath was the home of another 1962 newcomer to the PL, Leicester, who stepped down from the National League. Blackbird Road had a fine grandstand – the entrance was described by World Champion Jack Young as being like 'a super cinema' and extensive terracing. (John Somerville Collection.)

Team manager Ron Wilson (left) and Mike Parker (foreground) proudly present their new Provincial League team to the Blackbird Road patrons. Pictured on the tractor, l-r, are Vic White, John Poyser, Eric Hockaday, Bill Wainwright, Norman Hunter, Rick France and Slant Payling. (Alf Weedon/John Somerville Collection.)

season, with a team mostly composed of veterans and former northern juniors, was described by one media commentator as 'one of complete and utter rout'.

Whilst thousands were flocking to other Provincial tracks, notably Edinburgh and Wolverhampton, it was estimated that Leicester and Bradford between them had a combined weekly average attendance of little over 2000. And in the weeks following the end of the 1962 season it became obvious that Plymouth – despite a respectable mid-table finish and an unbeaten at home record – was likely to follow the two bottom-placed teams into (at least temporary) oblivion.

The Devon club had started the season with high hopes under promoter Bernard Curtiss, a flamboyant character with a handlebar moustache and a background in public relations. Curtiss gained some useful television publicity with a pre-season initiative to encourage young men with road bikes and a tendency to travel too fast on public roads to have a taste of speedway at a Pennycross training session.

The seven minute film, headlined *The Ton-Up Boys at Plymouth*, is, like the Neath footage, available on the BFI website to be watched free of charge. The film shows action shots of the tentative efforts around Pennycross of the road bikers and interviews with them and their mothers! There is also action footage of the Plymouth team men practising and interviews with Cliff Cox, Ivor Toms and Chris Julian, who were of the unanimous opinion that doing a ton on the road was more dangerous than racing speedway.

Provincial League action from Blackbird Road as Hunters' Vic White leads Middlesbrough's Eric Boocock and Eric Boothroyd into the first turn, with team-mate Slant Payling on the fence. Leicester finished next to bottom of the league, crowds did not meet expectations and the track closed at the end of the season. (John Simpson/John Somerville Collection.)

Bradford returned to the Provincial League for 1962, but with a new home. The Panthers, as they were known at the time, turned their back on the cavernous Odsal bowl and took up residence at the Greenfields greyhound stadium (aerial photo left) where the atmosphere suited the more modest crowds of the period. (Author's Collection.)

Bradford, bottom of the PL in 1960, again finished in the basement position in '62. Pictured is the Panthers' team, back row, l-r, Dennis Jenkins, Stuart Hickman, Reg Fearman (promoter), Tommy Roper. Kneeling, Wal Morton, Ray Day, Reg Duval and Geoff Pymar. (John Somerville Collection.)

Trouble in the champions' camp? On the back row of this team photograph Poole's Tim Bungay (left) and Geoff Mudge (right) appear to be having a disagreement, whilst sandwiched between them Tony Lewis and Ross Gilbertson are pretending to be unconcerned. Team manager Ron Hart seems not to have noticed. No problem at the front where, l-r, Roy Trigg, Norman Strachan, Bobby Croombs and Keith Whipp face the camera. (John Somerville Collection.)

As one of them comments to the interviewer, 'at least on the track everyone is going in the same direction'.

The chronicle of struggle and failure both at the top and bottom ends of the Provincial League table tends to overshadow the achievement of Poole in winning a second successive league championship. It was without doubt a considerable triumph achieved through careful team-building and the encouragement of relative newcomers – all qualities that have become typical of the management of the Wimborne Road track into the sport's modern era.

Poole faced the start of the new campaign with three certain team members in Geoff Mudge, Tony Lewis and Norman Strachan. The club persuaded Ross Gilbertson and Tim Bungay to stay on board, borrowed the extremely promising Roy Trigg from Wimbledon and added Bobby Croombs from New Cross, which had closed as a National League track at the end of 1961.

Ken Middleditch returned during a spell when the side was hit by injuries but the Pirates kept confidence in the development of Pete Munday and Brian Leonard, finished strongly and were worthy champions, five points ahead of Neath. The Dorset side's endorsement of the Provincial League was summed up at the end of the campaign by Jack Knott, from the club's management team, when he said:

> Poole has played a great part in the foundation of the Provincial League and, in the three seasons of its existence, has achieved the distinction of being runners-up in 1960 and champions in 1961 and 1962. Speedway has had a somewhat chequered career since 1928 but the quality of the sport and the courage of its participants has always kept the ship afloat.

> Today the Provincial League has infused such tremendous new life into the game that it now appears to be assuming a stability previously unknown. To say that a happy spirit prevailed at Poole in 1962 and, indeed, since the creation of the Provincial League, would be a gross understatement. Our riders, brilliantly led by Geoff Mudge, welded together in a purposeful co-partnership.

Midland sides Stoke and Cradley continued to please the fans at Sun Street and Dudley Wood despite not being in the running for PL honours in 1962. Stoke's rising star Colin Pratt leads Cradley idol Ivor Brown, who by this stage was the Provincial League rider the fans of other clubs loved to boo. (Peter Morrish/John Somerville Collection.)

Edinburgh was another PL track where the absence of a realistic bid for league honours did not dampen the spirits of the Old Meadowbank crowd. One of the entertainers in the Scottish capital was Wayne Briggs, younger brother of World Champion Barry. Wayne inspects the track as the crowds begin to file on to the terraces. (Ivan Stephenson/John Somerville Collection.)

It was not just administrators from with the PL set up who were recognising the effect the new competition had exerted upon speedway as a whole. In an anonymous review of the 1962 season the *Five Star Annual* had this to say (with the author probably being editor Cyril J Hart):

In just three seasons the Provincial League, at one time looked upon as speedway's poor relation, has grown into the major organisation operating in the United Kingdom. It is a success story, a period of fulfilment, a time in which young and imaginative minds have run riot and provided speedway in centres long since thought to be truly dead and buried.

Praise must be bestowed upon the PL administrators, but in all fairness we must not lose sight of the fact that while it is true they have expanded from the ten teams with which they started in 1960 to the 14 which will start 1963, they have also been concerned with no fewer than eight track closures. This is a high rate of exchange but whilst their policy enables more tracks to operate in a year than were in existence the previous year, credit for an expansionist outlook must still be theirs.

The number of Provincial League tracks again allowed a full overall programme, with the variety of visiting sides keeping the fans content. The season began with the regional league programme, with Wolverhampton taking a close-run Midland League with a margin of just two points over Cradley, followed by Leicester and Stoke.

Sheffield were clear winners of the five-team Northern League, with a five point lead over runners-up Middlesbrough. The Bears' eight points were also achieved by next placed Edinburgh and Newcastle, with Bradford, whose problems began early in the season, recording just one win.

Poole, overall PL champions, also triumphed in the four-team Southern League, having a 12 point winning margin over Exeter and Plymouth, with Neath at the bottom, also with just one point – making their later performances in the main PL competition even more remarkable.

The Provincial League Knock-out Cup, raced over a 16-heat format with seven man teams, was won by Exeter, with a 106-86 aggregate victory over Stoke in a two-legged final. The Potters, who had beaten Poole 49-47 at Sun Street in a one-off semi-final raced at home in the first leg and established a 24 point lead over the Falcons. Colin Pratt led the Stoke charge with a 15 point maximum with good backing from Pete Jarman with 14 points and Ken Adams with ten. Len Silver led the Exeter scorers with 13 points.

In the return match at the County Ground Stoke were effectively blown away. Five home riders reached double figures and a sixth scored nine as the Falcons rattled up 70 points, with the Potters managing just 26 in reply, with Jarman (ten points) the only visitor in double figures.

Riders in the shrunken National League found it hard to get sufficient bookings outside club, World Championship and other major individual events. Some of the NL's lesser lights gained additional rides by taking part in Provincial League versus National League 'test matches', which in 1962 were staged at Wolverhampton, Newcastle and Stoke, and which the PL triumphed 2-1.

PL riders also had other 'tests' in the shape of Britain versus Overseas matches, at Poole, Cradley, Edinburgh, Exeter and Middlesbrough, with Britain winning the final match at Cleveland Park to take the series 3-2.

In the area of individual events in 1962 there were World Championship qualifying round at each Provincial League track, again contested not just by PL riders but also featuring a number of NL men. These events led to a Provincial Final for sixteen qualifiers, staged at Wolverhampton and won by Peter Vandenberg of Southampton. Five other riders, Jimmy Squibb, Doug Templeton, Brian Craven, Gil Goldfinch and Trevor Redmond qualified for the second round of the completion, competing against the cream of the National League. Brian Craven and Peter Vandenberg made it through to the semi-finals.

Len Silver of Exeter won the Provincial League Riders' Championship Final at Belle Vue, whilst all the PL tracks staged rounds in the World Championship, with the sixteen overall top scorers qualifying for the

The Provincial League Riders' Championship round at Exeter in August 1962 was the first speedway meeting watched by the author. Len Silver won the round, with Pete Lansdale second, while local favourite Eric Howe provided plenty of entertainment. (Author's Collection.)

Provincial Final at Wolverhampton. This was won by Peter Vandenberg, with five others, Jimmy Squibb, Doug Templeton, Brian Craven, Gil Goldfinch and Trevor Redmond going forward to round two where they joined the National League men.

Brian Craven, and Peter Vandenberg as reserve, made it through to the three semi-finals, at Wimbledon, Southampton and Norwich,

In the popular Silver Sash match-race championship several riders twice successfully defended their title after an initial win, with Ivor Brown of Cradley the first to withstand three challenges before losing. Between 12 May and 27 June Poole's Tony Lewis embarked upon a remarkable run of defeating ten successive challenges.

Journalist Peter Oakes, still happily very active in speedway today, summed up the PL's 1962 season with the comment:

> Three seasons have come and gone. The new league – frowned on by some in its early stages – has struggled to take root. Now it is growing steadily.

Family influences were also to the fore in this Wolverhampton line-up from the period. In the white overalls bottom right is Chris Sweetman, the Wolves' mascot, standing in front of his father Tommy. Pictured l-r are mechanical wizard Howard Cole Senior, Les Jenkins, Derek Strutt, Ernie Baker, Cyril Francis, Graham Warren, an unkown mechanic, Tommy Sweetman, Howard Cole Senior's son, also Howard (then known as Kid Bodie) and Bill Bridgett (Promoter). On the machine is Vic Ridgeon. (John Simpson/ John Somerville Collection.)

Opposite: *In the era before strict health and safety procedures, the pits could occasionally have a family atmosphere. Stoke's Ron Sharp reclaims his helmet from his son, watched by team-mate Colin Pratt. (Reg Fearman Collection.)*

Chapter 10

1963: DISPUTES, FAREWELLS AND MAUGER'S RETURN

The on-track rivalry between West Midland teams Wolverhampton and Stoke ended in the Potters initially topping the PL table. Wolverhampton lodged a protest and were awarded the title by the Control Board (details in this chapter). Competition between the two sides had been fierce all season as illustrated by this fine action shot of the up-and-coming Rick France (Wolves) and veteran Ken Adams (Stoke). (Peter Morrish/ John Somerville Collection.)

FOR the speedway newshounds (at the time), and for the sport's historians (as the years between have unfolded), the Provincial League's fourth season had just about everything to offer. The league began with a record 14 tracks, exactly double the number competing in the National League, the sport's first tier and home to some of the world's finest riders, but seemingly unable to reverse an alarming decline in strength.

As the months progressed, the headlines just kept coming. It was the year the 'Provincial' League went metropolitan, welcoming into its ranks for the first time teams from London, in the shape of another revival for New Cross and the return of speedway to Hackney Wick after a quarter of a century. The league extended its reach in the South West, with Cornish track St Austell seeing league speedway for the first time in a decade whilst Long Eaton, a long-closed Midland centre, also came back to life.

On the individual rider front the 1963 season saw the return to British speedway of Ivan Mauger. Quietly at first, and initially on borrowed equipment, the New Zealander laid a firm foundation for his stellar career, and became *the* man to beat on the Provincial League circuit.

Although a minority of the 1963 PL tracks followed the pattern of the three previous seasons and failed to attract really big attendances, the competition as a whole was an

Wolves won the league title after succeeding in reversing the result of a defeat at Middlesbrough. Bears' rider John Mills (pictured here in Long Eaton colours), adjudged by the Speedway Control Board to have been improperly registered, appears to be thoroughly fed up with the whole affair! (John Simpson/John Somerville Collection.)

obvious success, and to the average fan on the terraces everything in the garden seemed rosy. The only shadow on the horizon was the continuing atmosphere of distrust between the Provincial and National League promoters who, down to just seven tracks and with the threat of re-development hanging over at least two of their most successful venues, were struggling to stay viable.

There was even dissent within the PL ranks, with a bitter dispute between former partners Mike Parker and Reg Fearman, settled only by legal action and the threat by the sport's authorities to withhold licences to operate unless a solution was reached. For a while too Parker was also at odds with his fellow Provincial League promoters, who temporarily expelled him from their Association, the issue at stake being a disagreement over the signing of riders for Wolverhampton.

At the start of the season the break-up of the Parker-Fearman partnership had been dubbed the 'outbreak of the silent war' by the sport's top commentator, Eric Linden, founder and leading columnist of *Speedway Star*. Linden predicted in April that matches

*The Wolves celebrate
their victory. Pictured,
l-r, Jim Bond, Bill
Bridgett, Michael Beale
(team manager), Tommy
Sweetman, Mike Parker,
Cyril Francis, Dave
Hemus, Pete Adams,
Ernie Baker. In front is
mascot Chris
Sweetman. (Mark
Sawbridge.)*

*Despite being denied
league championship
medals Stoke riders Pete
Jarman (left) and Colin
Pratt had plenty of high
points to remember from
the 1963 season,
representing their
country at Provincial
League level. (John
Somerville Collection.)*

between Parker's teams – Wolverhampton, Newcastle and newcomers Hackney – and those controlled by Fearman – Stoke, Middlesbrough and Long Eaton – would make the sparks fly. But even Linden, with an acute nose for speedway, could not have predicted the eventual outcome.

When the season got underway it soon became obvious that the contest between Wolverhampton and Stoke, with less than 40 miles separating the two West Midland centres, was going to match the intense Black Country rivalry between Wolves and Cradley Heath, given the extra edge generated by the Parker-Fearman clash. It was a thriller of a campaign, with at the end only four points separating the champions from the side in sixth place.

When the teams got down to business on the track there was never a great deal in it on the six occasions the two sides met, in the PL, the Midland League and in challenge matches. With so many teams competing in 1963, the Provincial sides faced each other just twice in league clashes, as opposed to the four matches against each opponent raced in the National League that year.

Each side won its home Provincial League fixture, Wolves having a reasonably comfortable 43-35 victory at Monmore in May, whilst it was more or less the same scenario in the crunch match at Sun Street at the end of September, with Stoke winning 42-36. It was the final PL match of the season for both the Potters and the Wolves. Stoke were announced as champions at the end of the meeting and the home fans went home celebrating the Potters' first title success since winning (racing as Hanley) the National League Division Three championship in 1949.

It was not the end of the story. On 1 August Wolves had been narrowly defeated 40-38 by one of Reg Fearman's teams, Middlesbrough, at Cleveland Park. A Middlesbrough newcomer, John Mills enjoyed a reasonably good night for a relatively inexperienced rider, scoring five paid six points, with two second places and a crucial third behind his team-mate in heat eleven.

Although no objection to Mills' inclusion in the Bears' team had been raised by Wolverhampton at the time, it was discovered that Mills, officially a Rayleigh rider, had been improperly registered by Middlesbrough. Wolves entered an objection, the Control Board upheld their case, and Mills' points were deducted, giving victory in the match and in the league, to Wolverhampton. Stoke, who had originally topped the final table, were relegated to the runners-up slot.

The Potters', not surprisingly, were furious and so was Eric Linden, living up to his reputation as a hard-hitting, plain-spoken columnist. He devoted his entire page three comment article to the issue, writing:

Wolves also made headlines when the grandstand at Monmore Green was destroyed by fire in August. Speedway continued, with fans on the home straight terrace separated from the twisted wreckage by barriers. (John Somerville Collection.)

The impressive stand which replaced the old building is still a distinctive speedway landmark in the twenty-first century. The stand and the terrace is now the only available spectator accommodation at Monmore. (Author.)

The sport welcomed back one of its iconic clubs for 1963. The Provincial League version of the New Cross Rangers are pictured in traditional pose on the tractor. L-r, Reg Reeves, Jim Squibb, Bob Dugard, Eddie Reeves, Geoff Penniket, Des Lukehurst, Stan Stevens. (John Somerville Collection.)

Opposite: Bob Dugard, seen here wearing the Rangers' famous Maltese Cross emblem, was a son of pioneer rider and Eastbourne promoter Charlie Dugard. Bob's son Martin, grandsons Kelsey and Connor and Bob's brother John have also raced speedway over the years. (Ivan Stephenson/John Somerville Collection.)

It would be failing in my duty not to report that in my opinion Wolverhampton are the luckiest team ever to win a league title. You only have to look at the points scored to judge. Wolverhampton, placed first by the Control Board, had more points scored against them than they themselves scored – 906 for, 954 against. Yet every other team down to Hackney, who finished fourth from the bottom, scored more than they had scored against them.

In truth, Wolves were no championship outfit. They won because they kept a clear home record and managed a few away points. They won because there was not an outstanding team in the league – and a damned good job for that too. They won in the end because a crippled team (Middlesbrough) signed a rider no other side wanted and used him as the three heat leaders they had at the start of the season were all out of action at the same time.

Linden did not criticise the Speedway Control Board, saying he had no doubt that if the Board believed Mills had not been properly signed by Middlesbrough, then that was indeed the case, but he added:

Just as I have no doubt at all that, on moral grounds, Wolves should not have squawked to win on paper a league title they could not win on the track.

Stoke's fans were already reeling from the news that the Sun Street stadium was under threat of being sold to developers. The final meeting at the venue took place on 26 October with a three-way challenge for the Harjacmor Trophy between the Potters, Wolverhampton and Long Eaton. It was no doubt only small consolation to the followers of the Potters that their team won the trophy with 34 points to the 19 scored by both Wolverhampton and Long Eaton.

The Harjacmor Trophy was donated by three speedway journalists, Cyril J Hart (HAR), Howard Jacobi (JAC) and Peter Morrish (MOR). It was to be ten years before speedway

Hackney raced in National League Divisions One and Two in the middle and late 1930s but did not re-open post war until Mike Parker reintroduced the sport to Waterden Road in 1963. Pictured above, back row, l-r, Trevor Hedge, Jim Heard, Pete Sampson, Colin McKee, John Poyser, Malcolm Simmons, Mike Parker. Front row, kneeling, Ronnie Rolfe (left) and Tich Read. Norman Hunter on the machine. (John Somerville Collection.)

A dirty night at Newcastle, and a long journey home to come for a defeated Hackney team. The visitors made a good start when Norman Hunter headed home Brian Craven. Hunter was top scorer with 12 points from six rides for Hackney. (Spencer Oliver/John Somerville Collection.)

St Austell returned to league speedway in 1963 and signed World Finalist Ray Cresp as a spearhead. The Gulls' team pictured above is as follows, back row, l-r, Ray Cresp, Glyn Chandler, Fred Powell, Graham Hambly, Kneeling, l-r, Trevor Redmond, George Major, Ray Wickett and Chris Julian. (Sally Chandler.)

was to be seen in the Potteries again, with a side initially named after the location for a new track in the area, at Chesterton (Loomer Road).

Wolves, despite acquiring the league title, had experienced a season of decidedly mixed fortunes. Crowds flocked to Monmore Green – reportedly 11,000 at the first meeting of 1963 and a season's average of 6000 – but the venue lost its main grandstand to a raging fire during the campaign. The promotion kept speedway going nevertheless, with barriers separating the crowds on the terracing from the twisted wreckage of the former structure's steel frame. The greyhound promotion was less fortunate, being forced to close temporarily due to the fire having destroyed all their records.

St Austell's return to league racing lasted for just the 1963 season, although the crowds visible in the background of this start line shot appear to be substantial. Getting away from the tapes in a Provincial League match against Stoke at the Cornish Stadium are, l-r, Ron Sharpe (Stoke), Mike Keen (St Austell), Ken Adams (Stoke) and Glyn Chandler (St Austell). (Sally Chandler.)

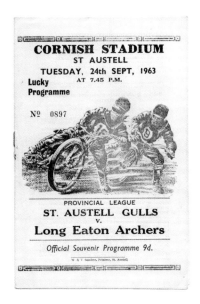

CORNISH STADIUM
ST AUSTELL
TUESDAY, 24th SEPT, 1963
AT 7.45 P.M.
Lucky
Programme

No 0897

PROVINCIAL LEAGUE
ST. AUSTELL GULLS
v.
Long Eaton Archers

Official Souvenir Programme 9d.

The battle between the Potters and the Wolves tended to overshadow the attempt by Poole to record a hat-trick of Provincial League title victories. The Pirates finished third, two points behind Wolverhampton and a point behind Stoke in the revised league table. Poole's 28 points was equalled by Sheffield and surprise packets St Austell in fourth and fifth spots, whilst sixth-placed Newcastle had 27 points.

If a lion's share of the headlines concerned the rivalry between Parker and Fearman and their respective teams, that did not mean that there was little of consequence and interest happening elsewhere, particularly in London. When New Cross had pulled out mid-season in 1953, it heralded a steady decline in the sport's fortunes. Johnnie Hoskins brought racing back to the Old Kent Road in 1959, on an open licence, and the Rangers took their place in the National League for 1960 and 1961.

The National League's tide was flowing against Hoskins' brave venture and there was no speedway at New Cross in 1962. Wally Mawdsley and Pete Lansdale had revived Exeter with considerable success, running the County Ground alongside Rayleigh in 1961 and on its own in '62. For 1963 the duo decided upon three tracks, Rayleigh, Exeter and New Cross, with the latter team operating for the first time ever in the lower tier of British speedway,

If a New Cross revival was a gamble, the other London track to join the Provincial League, Hackney was just as much a shot in the dark. The East London track had been part of British speedway for the five seasons before the outbreak of World War Two, running for two years in the National League, competing against New Cross, the more

The fourth new track to be welcomed to the PL in 1963 (if the returning Rayleigh could be counted as a newcomer) was Long Eaton. The Derbyshire side pictured above lacks its number one rider, Australian quiet man Charlie Monk, who often refused to be included in team shots early in his career. Not so camera shy are, back row l-r, Gil Goldfinch, Ron Wilson (team manager), Ken Vale and Danny Dunton. Kneeling, l-r, Bluey Scott, Slant Payling and Vic White. Also missing from the shot is Jon Erskine. (John Somerville Collection.)

The Archers' first season in the PL saw the debut of the track's finest discovery, future World Cup star Ray Wilson, son of team-manager Ron. (John Simpson/John Somerville Collection.)

Speedway history in the making. Ivan Mauger prepares for his first match for Newcastle on his 1963 return to the UK. Pictured on the pre-match parade at Cleveland Park, Middlesbrough are, l-r Brian Craven, Mike Watkin, Ivan Crozier, Ivan Mauger, Pete Kelly. (Spencer Oliver/ John Somerville Collection.)

glamorous Wembley, Harringay and Wimbledon and East End neighbours West Ham. Like Northern and Midland tracks Leeds and Nottingham, Hackney did not resurface after the war.

It is time to turn to the fortunes of individuals on the track in 1963 and to focus in particular on Ivan Mauger, last met in Chapter Four, returning home to New Zealand after finding it hard to break into the shrunken British speedway scene.

As a teenage fan in 1963, looking forward to watching my first full season of speedway racing in my home town of Long Eaton and an avid consumer of *Speedway Star* each week, I can only recall being fairly indifferent to the news of the return of a rider who, by all accounts, had failed to pull up many trees during his previous spell in the UK. Any British fans who shared my indifference were soon to start to think again.

Mauger, barely nineteen years of age when he made the decision to follow his wife Raye back home to New Zealand in the autumn of 1958, after Ronnie Greene at Wimbledon had made it clear that he was not prepared to pay for Ivan's family to return to Britain for the following season, was now a mature man with much more experience of both speedway and life than he had possessed on his first arrival in Britain in 1957.

The lack of interest in Mauger shown by Britain's National League promoters was, with hindsight, to prove much more of a turning point in his career than he or anyone else could have realised at the time.

Back in New Zealand, after a reunion with his family, Ivan persevered with his racing ambitions and made the shorter trip to Australia, together his brother Trevor, best friend Bernie LaGrosse and another friend, Ivan Crozier.

For the 1960-61 season Mauger was signed by Adelaide promoter Kym Bonython to ride at the Rowley Park track in the South Australian city. A key player in what became known as Ivan's Australian apprenticeship was his discovery of a mentor in the form of the rider Mauger had always idolised, Jack Young, World Champion in 1951 and 1952, whose home track was Rowley Park.

New Zealand speedway journalist and writer Tracy Holmes firmly believes that the rejection of Mauger by British promoters at the end of 1958 proved a major blessing:

Opposite: Ivan Mauger, a Diamond in the making in 1963. (Ivan Stephenson/ John Somerville Collection.)

As it turned out, it was the best thing that could have happened, because it led eventually to Ivan going to Australia. His friendship with Jack Young did him more good than any experience racing in the leagues in Britain could have done. In the years between leaving the UK in 1958 and his return five years later, Young taught him everything there was to know, and Ivan absorbed the lot.

So when Mike Parker signed him for Newcastle for the 1963 season Ivan was more than ready for the task ahead!

The contrast between the raw novice of 1957 and the rider of 1963 was substantial. Ivan had won the Victorian and Queensland state championships in 1962, as well as the Australian Long Track title. He was also second in the 1962 Australian Solo Championship, finishing behind the experienced New South Wales man Bob Sharp.

Mauger always gave full credit to the role played by Jack Young in laying the groundwork for his own spectacular World Championship success. Young told Mauger that it was not necessarily the fastest rider who won the World title but the rider who at the end of the meeting had scored the most points. To reach that position the successful rider had to also concentrate on conserving his machine and getting the best out of it throughout the meeting, a lesson Ivan never forgot.

Newcastle was an exciting place to be in 1963. Pictured roaring away from the tapes in a Diamonds-Edinburgh Monarchs clash are, l-r, Doug Templeton (Monarchs), Ivan Mauger (Diamonds), Jimmy Tannock (Monarchs) and Brian Craven (Diamonds). (Spencer Oliver/John Somerville Collection.)

Young added that it didn't in the end amount to much if a rider led a race until half a lap from home only to discover that he had pushed his bike beyond its limits and failed to finish.

When Mauger's thoughts turned to giving British speedway another chance, his initial attempts to find a club drew no response. His letters to Ronnie Greene at Wimbledon and to Charles Ochiltree at Coventry were not answered. Having signed contracts at Wimbledon for both 1957 and 1958, Ivan's name still appeared on the Plough Lane retained list and Mike Parker had to work hard to sign Mauger for Newcastle.

After a relatively slow start Ivan began to score heavily for the Diamonds and there were those in British speedway who voiced the opinion that he should not be allowed to race in the lower division. Mauger himself found it ironic that promoters who had failed to reply to his letters a few months before now scrambled to include him in National League sides as the 1963 season progressed. The record books show appearances for Oxford, eventual champions Southampton and, supreme irony of all, Wimbledon!

Where individual events were concerned, the name on everyone's lips by the end of the 1963 season was Ivan Mauger, who crowned his comeback year by winning the Provincial League Riders Championship Final at Belle Vue, ahead of Sheffield's Jack Kitchen and Poole's Ross Gilbertson.

Mauger also enjoyed success in the earlier rounds of the World Championship, winning qualifiers at Newcastle and Wolverhampton. Ivan and his arch rival Ivor Brown each dropped just a single point in their two meetings, but the star of the round was Kitchen, who recorded two maximums. Eight riders qualified for the Provincial Final at Edinburgh, with Mauger again dropping just one point.

Eight riders went through to the second round but Mauger, still not quite the finished product at the highest level, failed to go through to round three, for which Doug Templeton of Edinburgh was the only PL qualifier.

Before Ivan Mauger's 1963 return the role of top man in Provincial League racing, and the reputation as being the rider opposition fans loved to boo, had fallen to Ivor Brown of Cradley Heath, despite his lack of success in the PL Riders Championship finals.

At the end of the 1963 campaign Ivor was left scratching his head, having lost the title of the main target of the boo boys to his Kiwi rival. Ivor said at the time: 'I'm not really doing anything different and I feel I am riding just as hard as I ever did.'

Speedway Star's round-up of the 1963 season's statistics provided some consolation for Brown, ranking him as the league's top man based on points scored in official team

The excitement was generated by the packed crowd at Brough Park for the Newcastle-Edinburgh match. The Monarchs fans are well represented on the home straight terracing. (Spencer Oliver/John Somerville Collection.)

*Newcastle provided a
pipe band to welcome
visitors Edinburgh to
Brough Park.*

*Completing a hugely
successful return to
speedway Ivan Mauger
won the Provincial
League Riders'
Championship at Belle
Vue. Pictured l-r, Ivan
Mauger, Scottish
Speedway Queen Dae
Strachan, Jack Kitchen,
Ross Gilbertson.
(Spencer Oliver/John
Somerville Collection.)*

matches, ahead of Jimmy Squibb of New Cross and Exeter, George Hunter of Edinburgh
and, in fifth place, Ivan Mauger.

At the start of this chapter reference was made to the festering dispute between the
National League and the Provincials. As the 1963 season drew to a close and the Nationals
faced up to the loss of Southampton, the promoters of the senior section, with the backing
of the Speedway Control Board, tried to force the Provincial League Promoters to agree to
the promotion of PL champions Wolverhampton to make up the numbers.

Mike Parker dug in his heels, preferring to remain in the Provincial League. Despite
the league's own internal disputes, his fellow promoters closed ranks and refused to give
in. The next chapter will examine the far-reaching consequences of speedway's civil war.

Chapter 11

1964: 'BLACKED' BUT STILL TRIUMPHANT!

WOULD the Provincial League promoters really carry out their threat and run the 1964 season outside the jurisdiction of the Speedway Control Board and the Auto-Cycle Union (ACU)? Or would the differences between the National League and the PL camp be settled in time for the new season?

In the months leading up to the scheduled start of the 1964 campaign there were not infrequent suggestions in the speedway press that peace *was* about to break out,. Respected media pundits such as Eric Linden needed to constantly hedge their bets, the only sensible thing to do when the situation was liable to change virtually overnight.

There were other questions too. Would sufficient riders choose loyalty to the PL bosses who for four successful campaigns had provided them with a living, or would a significant number prefer to stay legitimate and obey the instructions of the sport's authorities? This question was of particular relevance to the substantial number of riders whose motorcycle racing activities embraced not just speedway but other branches of the sport, notably grass track racing.

In reality the vast majority of Provincial League riders had virtually no choice if they wished to continue in the sport. There had been all too few opportunities for them in the days before the launch of the PL, and the National League had dwindled in the early 1960s to a bare minimum of tracks.

When Southampton's Bannister Court Stadium was sold for development at the end of 1963 and it became obvious that the PL was unwilling to lose any tracks to the higher

Welcome to the new season! Once it became apparent that the Provincial League was going to operate successfully in 1964 outside the jurisdiction of the speedway authorities the Control Board paid for an advert in the sport's media informing riders at PL clubs that they were suspended. (Author's Collection.)

ADVERTISER'S ANNOUNCEMENT

NOTICE TO ALL SPEEDWAY RIDERS IN THE 'PROVINCIAL LEAGUE'

Pursuant to the Statement published in the issue of "Speedway Star & News" of the 15th February, 1964 it was decided that personal notification be given to all riders riding for the "Provincial League" advising them that they risk suspension if they continue to ride for their present promoters. In some cases communications to riders whose addresses were not known, were sent to the riders c/o the track, but some of these have been returned unopened, and it would appear that the contents are not known to the riders. Accordingly, notice is now given to all riders now riding on the undermentioned tracks that they have been suspended by the Board.

Cradley Heath, Edinburgh, Exeter, Glasgow, Hackney, Long Eaton, Middlesbrough, Newcastle, Newport, Poole, Rayleigh, Sheffield, Sunderland and Wolverhampton.

THE SPEEDWAY CONTROL BOARD.

This space has been paid for by the Control Board to ensure, as far as is possible, that riders will be aware of their position.

Many riders in the early spring of 1964 hesitated before committing themselves to an unlicensed league. Ivor Brown of Cradley (left) was absent from the first meeting raced under the 'blacked' Provincial regime, whilst former Cradley team-mate Stan Stevens, opted to join newly-reopened side West Ham in the legitimate National League. (Spencer Oliver/John Somerville Collection.)

league and a merger between the two competitions was unlikely in the near future, the senior section promoters were forced to revive West Ham as a joint effort, or lose their viability entirely.

And what would be the attitude of the fans, the paying customers? At the start of the 1964 season I was still a teenage fan and the only news item during the 1963-64 close season that I regarded as being of prime interest and importance was the announcement that my hometown track Long Eaton would compete again.

The 1964 PL was to consist of 13 tracks, with a revived Glasgow White City and north-eastern newcomers Sunderland replacing yo-yo club Rayleigh. Out of the league were Stoke, where the Sun Street track had also fallen victim to the developers, St Austell, returning to non-league status and New Cross, a mid-season closure during the course of the previous season.

Of these 13 tracks only one, Poole, had a fairly recent link (as members in 1959), with the National League. For the supporters at the remaining 12 venues, speedway *was* the Provincial League. Parker, Fearman, the Hoskins, Mawdsley and Lansdale and the other promoters were *the* people who had restored (or in the case of Newport had created) their weekly speedway fix. They were hardly likely to abandon their home track and, where possible, transfer their loyalty to the nearest NL centre.

There was nevertheless a good deal of tension in the air when the first meetings of 1964 approached. The fixture that would turn the PL threat into a true revolt was scheduled for the County Ground, Exeter, on 16 March. A crowd of around 4700 turned out, including

Ivan Mauger (left), already with international ambitions, also held back from the PL for a short while until, like Ivor Brown, his opponent above, deciding to stay in the league, with Newcastle. (Spencer Oliver/John Somerville Collection.)

a good number of other Provincial League promoters anxious to see at first hand what would happen.

Exeter skipper Len Silver had personally telephoned every member of the Falcons team to make sure they were onside, and they all arrived ready to race. On the other side of the pits the situation was very different. Opponents Cradley Heath's top man Ivor Brown, Eric Hockaday and John Hart were absent from the line-up, still trying to make up their minds which way to jump.

The scheduled Provincial League fixture was changed to a Challenge Match, with Ross Gilbertson and Tim Bungay of Poole and Newport signing Alby Golden guesting for the Heathens. Exeter won the match 45-33, with Silver, Jimmy Squibb and Alan

Mrs Boocock's boys found themselves on different sides of the great speedway divide in 1964. Nigel (left) was a mainstay of National League Coventry whilst Eric, after first signing for NL Belle Vue, then returned to ride for Middlesbrough in the Provincial League. (Ivan Stephenson/John Somerville Collection.)

1964 again saw the almost inevitable game of musical chairs before the PL season started with three teams leaving only to be replaced by three newcomers to the league. The PL's second Welsh team, Newport raced at Somerton Park, home of the local Football League club. Pictured is the back straight and the very tight corners. (John Somerville Collection.)

Glasgow White City was an extremely well-appointed big city greyhound stadium, with impressive spectator facilities. (Peter Colvin.)

Cowland in fine form for the Falcons. Tim Bungay was top scorer for an understandably subdued Cradley.

One man undecided what to do at this point was Ivan Mauger, the PL's hottest property, who had been booked for second half match races. Mauger declined to ride, but won the respect of the PL camp by driving all the way from his Manchester base to Exeter to explain his position in person to the Falcons management.

Those lined-up behind the National League and the sport's authorities claimed that Cradley's inability to turn out a meaningful side, the use of guest riders and the fact that the advertised league match did not take place counted against any claims by the PL of success. It was suggested that 'speedway-starved fans' might turn up for one meeting but might not take the risk again of watching a completely different match to the one advertised.

On the following Saturday evening the action moved from Glorious Devon to the Black Country and Cradley's Dudley Wood Stadium. Although the second round of the opening clash between Cradley and Exeter was necessarily now just the second leg of a challenge match, rather than the intended league fixture, it proved to be a momentous night for the Provincial League.

Exeter skipper Len Silver had already proved to be a key element in ensuring that the very first PL match got underway, by rallying the support of the Falcons' riders. At Cradley a few days after that meeting he was again at the very centre of things. The story of what happened in the Black Country is best told in Len's own words.

I was captain of Exeter at the time and, probably because I was a rebel by nature, fully agreed with the idea of operating a 'Black' League. At the time the pay rates in the league were on a sliding scale depending on your score, from ten shillings (50p) to a maximum of £1 (ten points or more to get paid at that rate).

Sunderland's Bolden Stadium still staged greyhound racing in 2020, although the cover over the home straight spectator area has been removed. (John Somerville Collection.)

The initial matches for that season, Exeter v Cradley Heath and Cradley Heath v Exeter, were picked because it was known that I had some personal influence with the riders and had spent many hours on the phone persuading them to take part. The Provincial League's top man, Ivan Mauger, and others, were sitting on the fence!

On the evening of the Cradley match I asked to meet Morris Jephcott, the Heathens' promoter, before the racing began. My wish was granted and to my surprise, when I entered the room to meet him, almost all of the Provincial promoters were there, most of whom I knew personally as they were ex-riders.

I asked that the pay rate be reviewed so that the sliding scale was dropped and all riders to be paid at £1 per point and £1 per start. I remember Morris Jephcott asking: 'If we do not agree, will the riders ride ?', to which I lied in my teeth and said, 'No they will not' (most of the riders did not even know I was negotiating for them!)

With no further delay, Jephcott declared: 'Then we agree to the rate'. The rest of those there nodded in agreement and I went back to the pits with the good news for

The three new tracks enjoyed different fortunes. Newport finished in fourth place in the league, enjoyed very large crowds at home and boosted attendances elsewhere with their travelling support. The Wasps were a well turned-out team with a full squad pictured here. Standing, l-r, are Bob Hughes, Vic White, Geoff Pennikett, Jon Erskine, Dick Bradley, Peter Vandenberg, Fred Powell, Ray Harris. Kneeling are juniors Alan Jones and Peter Harris. Skipper Alby Golden is on the machine. (John Somerville Collection.)

Promoter Trevor Redmond drew his Glasgow Tigers' side in 1964 from far and wide. Hampshire-based Maury Mattingley (front row centre) flew to Scotland every week to race and Cornishman Chris Julian was more usually associated with clubs in the South West. On the track the Tigers finished at the foot of the PL. Pictured are, standing, l-r, Bill McMillan, Charlie Monk, Trevor Redmond, Bruce Ovenden, Terry Stone. Front row, l-r, Chris Julian, Maury Mattingley, Red Monteith. (Author's Collection.)

the riders. We rode the two matches in very cold and damp weather in front of very big crowds and the 'Black' league was off and running. Two days later, Ivan Mauger agreed to ride.

In the match at Cradley Ivor Brown, having signed his PL contract celebrated with a maximum, and John Hart was also in the side.

If it was Glasgow's misfortune to be bottom of the Provincial League, Sunderland's first taste of speedway was even less successful. The Saints raced just three PL matches and a handful of challenge matches and individual events before promoter Mike Parker pulled the plug. The team relied heavily on young Australasians and veterans. Pictured standing l-r are: Graham Coombes, Vic Ridgeon, Gordon Guasco, Jim Airey, Colin McKee, Dave Collins. On the bike is Ken Sharples. (John Somerville Collection.)

The only absentee on this occasion was Eric Hockaday, and he watched from the sidelines, signing his own contract as soon as the match finished, telling the *Speedway Star* reporter: 'I was holding back because I wanted to see what happened.' Cradley won the match 40-37 but Exeter took the tie on aggregate.

At this stage the Provincial League Promoters Association increased its membership to 18, admitting tracks at the time operating outside the league structure – Eastbourne, Plymouth, Rayleigh, St Austell and Weymouth – as open licence members. Of tracks in this category, only Rye House chose to line up with the National League.

One of the more curious aspects of the dispute was the initial attitude of the Speedway Riders Association (SRA). Whilst the Control Board took out paid advertising to warn licensed riders not to compete in the blacked Provincial League, the riders' trade union told its members not to ride in *any* league until the dispute between the two bodies was settled.

Veteran Ken Adams, a long-term member of the SRA, had moved to Long Eaton on Stoke's closure. Although taking the dispute seriously, he could not resist quipping: 'The

Control Board and the National League could not provide employment for every rider in the country. What would have happened if all the Provincial League riders had applied to the Control Board for re-allocation?'

Several promising Provincial riders *did* opt for the National League, notably Norman Hunter of Hackney, Colin Pratt, with Stoke in 1963, Eric Boocock of Middlesbrough and Ray Cresp of St Austell. Hunter and Cresp, who had raced for just one season in the PL and was a former World Finalist, stayed the whole season with the NL. Pratt, Boocock and others found they were losing financially and after a spell returned to the Provincial ranks.

Eric Boocock's decision to move into the National League had been influenced by a long chat with elder brother Nigel, the Coventry star. Eric told *Speedway Star:*

> Nigel convinced me that I should go into the National League with Belle Vue, and even though I did eventually return to the PL in some ways I still think he was right. After all, the promoters in the National League are mainly the men who kept the game going in the late 1950s. They must be sound, reliable sort of operators.
>
> Why am I back in the Provincial League? One word, MONEY. I simply can't earn enough in the NL to make ends meet.

Once the season began to settle down there were success stories to tell in both leagues. West Ham opened to a crowd estimated at 15,000 and 10,000 people were reported to have attended Newport's first meeting, with hundreds still pouring through the Somerton Park turnstiles when racing began.

As in so many bitter civil wars the backbiting at times became petty. At West Ham it was reported that press facilities had been withdrawn from Dave Stevens, who in addition to being a freelance journalist was also part-time secretary of the Provincial League Promoters Association. It was suggested that he had been banned from the press box because of his PL connection.

Provincial League promoters and riders were also required to pay at the turnstiles at the West Ham opener, although the PL insisted it would not retaliate!

The PL received a welcome endorsement from one of the most highly regarded administrators in speedway, Lt Colonel R Vernon C Brook, a former chairman of the Control Board. Lt-Col Brook accepted the post of judge for the Provincial League's new appeals court, which gave riders the opportunity to appeal against any punishments handed down by the league for breach of rules.

The completed Provincial League table at the end of the season represented a triumph for the competition. The league had proved that it could run efficiently outside the authority of the Control Board and the ACU. Newcastle, spearheaded by the inspirational

Ivan Mauger led Newcastle Diamonds to the Provincial League championship in 1964. Pictured l-r, Bill Andrew, Russ Dent, Mike Watkin, Mike Parker, Goog Allan, Ken Sharples, Peter Kelly. Ivan Mauger on machine. (Spencer Oliver/John Somerville Collection.)

1964 again brought individual as well as team success for Ivan Mauger. He won the Provincial League Riders' title for the second successive year, ahead of Charlie Monk (right) of Glasgow and Roy Trigg. (Hackney (Alf Weedon/John Somerville Collection.)

The Provincial League staged some international speedway during its 'black' season. Despite an 18 point maximum for Ivan Mauger at Newcastle, Scotland beat New Zealand 63-45 in April 1964. (Spencer Oliver/John Somerville Collection.)

A talking point in 1964 was the inclusion in the injury-hit Sheffield team for a Provincial League match against Long Eaton of veteran Wilf Jay and his two sons, Derek (left) and Alan. Wilf was fifty-one at the time of his one-match return. (Jay family.)

Ivan Mauger, won the title with a three-point margin over runners-up Hackney, whilst Wolverhampton overcame early season problems to finish third.

Inevitably the dispute between the warring factions was never far from the surface and, if anything, the bitterness increased as the season progressed towards a climax. The PL's big night out, the Riders' Championship Final, was the focus for an astonishing confrontation that provided a graphic illustration of the difference in status and outlook between Belle Vue and almost all other speedway managements.

Following the 1963 PLRC final at Hyde Road a verbal agreement had been reached between the Aces' management and the Provincial League promoters that the prestigious event would again be held again in Manchester in 1964. Unlike most speedway promotions, operating as tenants in a variety of venues, Belle Vue was part of the business empire controlled by Charles Forte, with interests in hotels, catering, exhibition venues and, in the case of the Hyde Road site, a zoo, amusement park, ballrooms and other leisure facilities in addition to the speedway stadium.

The Belle Vue management insisted on honouring its contract with the Provincial League promoters and the PLRC Final duly took place, creating a situation under which unlicensed riders raced on a licensed track. The Control Board suspended Belle Vue and the Aces team responded by riding challenge matches on PL tracks.

Ivan Mauger, who after enhancing his reputation by his behaviour towards the Exeter management at the end of March, quickly decided that his immediate future lay in the Provincial League, added a second successive victory in the PLRC to his league championship medal, averaging almost 12 points over the season in official matches, and also ended the season as the possessor of the Silver Sash. Running 'black' meant that all PL riders were barred from the World Championship but Ivan was to more than amply make up for that temporary disappointment in the future.

Inevitably, the Control Board and the National League promoters backed down over the Belle Vue issue. With so few tracks, and with a big question mark emerging over the future existence of Norwich, the NL simply could not afford to expel Belle Vue, a true jewel in their crown. It was becoming clear, above all to the National League managements, that the current state of affairs could not continue for much longer,

The RAC and the ACU at last conceded that the enquiry into the conduct of British speedway demanded by the Provincial League had to take place. The RAC appointed one of the country's most eminent lawyers, Lord Shawcross, a former Attorney General and the leading British prosecutor at the Nuremburg trials of Nazi war criminals, to conduct the enquiry and produce a report into the state of the sport in the UK.

Opposite: As the 1964 season drew to a close there were further headaches for National League strongmen Charles Ochiltree of Coventry and Ronnie Greene of Wimbledon, as Norwich followed Southampton into oblivion and the future of the senior division began to look extremely precarious. (Alf Weedon/John Somerville Collection.)

How the Speedway Star *reported the outbreak of peace in speedway's civil war and the plans for the new British League. (Author's Collection.)*

TWO   *SPEEDWAY STAR & NEWS, December 11, 1964*

ONE BIG LEAGUE

IT'S over bar the shouting. One big league. Eighteen tracks. Suspensions lifted. There, in a nutshell, is the speedway format for 1965.

The R.A.C. enquiry, headed by Lord Shawcross, announced its findings after a meeting on December 3, having heard recommendations from promoters from both the National and Provincial Leagues.

Now comes the big problem of sorting out team strengths. The promoters will endeavour to level team strengths themselves, but many teams will lose stars to help the needy.

Now take a look at the chief items.

to the rat race for the Swedish stars. The "keep-up-with-the-Joneses" attitude that may force some tracks to search for new talent in Scandinavia and on the Continent. Only time will tell whether the loss of Fundin, Knutsson, Sjosten and Nordin will have any lasting effect upon

speedway and, to be more precise, speedway support.
Why only 18 tracks?

The Control Board?
There will definitely be a new set-up at Pall Mall next year. Who will remain on the Board and who will be excluded has still to be decided, but what is certain is that the speedway promoters will definitely have a bigger say in things at Control Board level.

PAUL PARISH
reports on the findings of the R.A.C. enquiry

This is a tremendous victory for the Provincial League, who based much of their arguments

up to everyone concerned with the sport to make the loss easy to bear by providing racing both varied and attractive for the public.

The future of new tracks is undecided. In addition to the East Anglian sites of Littlechild and Thompson, the Provincial League have also said they have several new sites which may open. How they will be fitted in may well be one of the first duties of the new-look Control Board.

A young and ambitious Control Board will be a great asset. The fact that promoters will have a larger say in the running of the business should be a good thing, though I hope this will not lead to any petty jealousies.

Middlesbrough fans of all ages were disappointed when the Bears, who had experienced thinning crowds in 1964, were the only PL team which did not join the new British League for 1965, with Halifax effectively taking their place. (Spencer Oliver/John Somerville.)

What subsequently happened was reported extensively in the speedway media of the time and has since been explored and analysed extensively by the sport's historians and authors. My own book, *Speedway The Classic Era* (Halsgrove 2011 and reprinted in 2014 ISBN 9780857041043) contains a full account.

Just before Christmas 1964 the *Speedway Star* presented its readers with an early gift. The magazine's first news page carried a banner headline, in a type size double anything usually seen in the publication, simply saying, ONE BIG LEAGUE. The story below added:

It's over bar the shouting. One big league. Eighteen tracks, Suspensions lifted.
There in a nutshell is the speedway format for 1965.

The time had come to look towards what was to prove to be an exceptionally successful era for British speedway.

But it was also a time to look back on five years of the Provincial League and to reflect that the sport was entering a new era full of new found enthusiasm and confidence. Was this happy state of affairs due in great measure to the Provincial League and to the men who had the vision to bring the league into being and the faith to stick to their beliefs in 1964 when they were labelled as rebels?

Peter Morrish, there at the start of the Provincial League and still active today as announcer at Wolverhampton and actively involved in the organisation of the sport's official riders' points averages (the 'green sheets' which play such an important role in determining team places) is in no doubt about the role played by the PL, saying:

Speedway in the late 1950s was absolutely dead. The National League bosses had run out of ideas. There was a belief that they had all been in the sport for too long. The Provincial League *did* save speedway!

A taste of things to come. The British League gave Provincial discoveries like future Speedway World Cup winner Ray Wilson of Long Eaton a chance to gain experience against top men like Barry Briggs, who he is pictured leading at Station Road. (John Sumpter.)

Stoke rider/promoter Reg Fearman receives the Provincial League's Silver Sash in 1960. (Reg Fearman Collection.)

POSTSCRIPT

The foreword to this book was penned by Len Silver, Provincial League Riders' Champion in 1962 and today still very much involved with speedway as promoter at one of the sport's newest tracks.

The final words belong to another of speedway's great names, Reg Fearman, who in the pioneering year of 1960 was both promoter at Stoke and at the same time one of the Potters' leading riders.

Speedway racing had been in the doldrums for several years by the time 1960 came around. It was in the winter of 1959-1960 that like minded people, men who had experience of speedway racing in the 1940s and 1950s, got together in a flat in Manchester, owned by Mike Parker. Ten tracks emerged for that first season of the Provincial League, under the authority of the Speedway Control Board and eight of the ten promoters had previous experience either as riders or promoter/stadium owners.

The season opened with great enthusiasm. The 48% Entertainment Tax had long gone and the people who had sat around their televisions for five or six years were ready once again for outdoor entertainment. Speedway offered excellent entertainment, it was cheap and a great night out with some twenty races and in many cases interval attractions of various descriptions. It was the birth of the Swinging Sixties and it was certainly very much a fun time at the speedway in those first years of the PL.

Many of the ten teams in that first season encouraged young riders who had been practising riding speedway wherever they could. My promotion at Stoke was one that encouraged the novices. It was because of this the Speedway Control Board gave me permission to both promote and race for Stoke, where I could coach riders under real racing conditions.

Long-awaited stability for speedway arrived in 1965 with the amalgamation of the Provincial League (12 teams) and the National League with just 6, making a total of 18 tracks for the new British League. Fifteen years on in 1980 there were still 17 teams in the British League. As the figures clearly show, the National League was no longer viable. The Provincial League could have progressed alone, but the National League could have died.

Thankfully, common sense prevailed and the British League became a happy combination of the best of the two competitions.

Since then many stadiums have become property development sites but speedway racing still survives with new venues. History repeats itself with today 7 teams in the top tier and 12 teams in the second tier. Another amalgamation?

Reg Fearman

Statistical Appendix

1960 PROVINCIAL LEAGUE

Team	Mts	Won	Drn	Lst	For	Agn	Pts
Rayleigh	18	16	0	2	808	485	32
Poole	18	16	0	2	721	494	32
Bristol	18	15	0	3	750	538	30
Sheffield	18	9	0	9	585	632	18
Stoke	18	8	1	9	604	669	17
Cradley Heath	18	8	0	10	641	650	16
Yarmouth	18	7	0	11	612	595	14
Edinburgh	18	5	1	12	573	710	11
Liverpool	18	4	0	14	527	758	8
Bradford 'Panthers'	18	1	0	17	459	749	2

PL KNOCK-OUT CUP FINAL: Bristol 100 Rayleigh 89
PL RIDERS' CHAMPIONSHIP: Trevor Redmond (Bristol), 15 pts

1961 PROVINCIAL LEAGUE

Team	P	W	D	L	F	A	Pts
Poole	20	15	1	4	932½	622½	31
Plymouth	20	12	0	8	826	726	24
Stoke	20	12	0	8	811	737	24
Cradley Heath	20	11	1	8	781	777	23
Rayleigh	20	11	0	9	769	784	22
Edinburgh	20	10	1	9	784	767	21
Sheffield	20	10	0	10	782	772	20
Exeter	20	9	0	11	772½	777½	18
Wolverhampton	20	7	0	13	715	841	14
Middlesbrough	20	6	1	13	712½	839½	13
Newcastle	20	5	0	15	655½	897½	10

PL KNOCK-OUT CUP FINAL: Cradley Heath 102 Edinburgh 87
PL RIDERS' CHAMPIONSHIP: Reg Reeves (Rayleigh), 15 pts

1962 PROVINCIAL LEAGUE

Team	P	W	D	L	F	A	Pts
Poole	24	17	0	7	1081	780	34
Neath	24	14	1	9	970	896	29
Exeter	24	14	0	10	981	883	28
Stoke	24	14	0	10	949	916	28
Edinburgh	24	12	2	10	959	904	26
Plymouth	24	12	2	10	919	942	26
Sheffield	24	12	1	11	976½	889½	25
Cradley Heath	24	12	0	12	937	930	24
Newcastle	24	12	0	12	882½	976½	24
Wolverhampton	24	11	1	12	900½	960½	23
Middlesbrough	24	11	0	13	958	912	22
Leicester	24	6	0	18	826½	1036½	12
Bradford	24	5	1	18	775	1089	11

PL KNOCK-OUT CUP FINAL: Exeter 106 Stoke 86
PROVINCIAL LEAGUE RIDERS' CHAMPIONSHIP: Len Silver (Exeter)

1963 PROVINCIAL LEAGUE

Team	P	W	D	L	For	Agnst	Pts
Wolverhampton	24	15	1	8	906	954	31
Stoke	24	14	1	9	971½	895½	29
Poole	24	14	0	10	1004	867	28
Sheffield	24	14	0	10	986	802	28
St Austell	24	13	2	9	967	895	28
Newcastle	24	13	1	10	890	889	27
Exeter	24	12	1	11	985	882	25
Edinburgh	24	12	1	11	969½	896½	25
Cradley Heath	24	11	1	12	934	927	23
Hackney	24	10	1	13	875	990	21
Middlesbrough	24	9	2	13	881	980	20
Long Eaton	24	7	2	15	848	1009	16
Rayleigh	24	5	1	18	815	1045	11
New Cross	**Withdrew mid-season.**						

PL KNOCK-OUT CUP FINAL: Cradley Heath 109 Newcastle 82
PROVINCIAL LEAGUE RIDERS' CHAMPIONSHIP: Ivan Mauger (Newcastle)

1964 PROVINCIAL LEAGUE

Team	P	W	D	L	For	Agnst	Pts
Newcastle	22	17	0	5	966	747	34
Hackney	22	15	1	6	929	786	31
Wolverhampton	22	12	1	9	871	841	25
Newport	22	11	1	10	885	829	23
Edinburgh	22	10	2	10	884½	827½	22
Poole	22	10	1	11	834	882	21
Exeter	22	10	1	11	823	813	21
Sheffield	22	9	2	11	817½	818½	20
Middlesbrough	22	9	2	11	768	948	20
Cradley Heath	22	8	1	13	840	875	17
Long Eaton	22	8	0	14	781	931	16
Glasgow	22	6	2	14	805	906	14
Sunderland	**Withdrew mid-season.**						

PL KNOCK-OUT CUP FINAL: Newport 97 Cradley Heath 95
PL RIDERS' CHAMPIONSHIP: Ivan Mauger (Newcastle), 13 pts